David and Darcy

Here's to Maximizing
Your Return on Life!

ADVANCE PRAISE

"Writing and publishing a book about values has been a goal of yours for many years. I am so proud of the book (and relieved that is finished). I hope your readers will find me innocent on page 30."

~Stephen Reiches
Shari's husband

"In *Maximize Your Return on Life*, Shari empowers investors to make smart money decisions by focusing first on what's truly important to them—their core values. By asking the right questions and fully understanding what matters most to her clients, Shari delivers invaluable advice that helps them stay invested and stick to their long-term plans."

~David Booth
Founder and Executive Chairman Dimensional Fund Advisors

"Shari has consistently demonstrated her values-based philosophy in all aspects of her life—as a mother, wife, friend, business owner, and non-profit leader. I've seen firsthand the ways she shares her time, expertise, and creativity with our synagogue, and I'm delighted that she has shared her approach in *Maximize Your Return on Life*."

~Karen Isaacson
President, Beth Emet The Free Synagogue

"As Vice Chair for the Illinois State Board of Investments, Shari excelled at breaking down complex ideas and getting to the heart of what really matters for institutional investors. *Maximize Your Return on Life* provides a roadmap for how to do the same when we make personal decisions on spending our time and money. Whether it's a boardroom table decision affecting billions of dollars, or a kitchen table budgeting decision, Shari's advice is spot on."

~Johara Farhadieh
Executive Director and Chief Investment Officer
The Illinois State Board of Investments

"Stop with the advice already, Mom! We get it… Just kidding! We love you and your advice."

~Maddie and Isabel Reiches
Shari's children

MAXIMIZE
YOUR RETURN ON LIFE

Invest Your Time and Money
in What You Value Most

MAXIMIZE
YOUR RETURN ON LIFE

Invest Your Time and Money
in What You Value Most

SHARI GRECO REICHES

WINDY CITY
PUBLISHERS

MAXIMIZE
YOUR RETURN ON LIFE
Invest Your Time and Money in What You Value Most

Windy City Publishers
Chicago, IL
info@windycitypublishers.com

Published in the United States of America

ISBN#:
978-1-953294-09-8

Library of Congress Control Number:
2021905435

WINDY CITY PUBLISHERS
CHICAGO

www.windycitypublishers.com

"You can have anything you want,
but you can't have everything you want."

~Dante A. Greco
Founder and CEO
Bank of Highwood and New Century Bank
(and my father)

CONTENTS

MAXIMIZE
Your Return on Time

MAXIMIZE
Your Return on Investing and Financial Planning

MAXIMIZE
Your Return for Your Loved Ones

MAXIMIZE
Your Return with Gratitude

How Will You
MAXIMIZE
Your Return on Life?

FOREWORD

L ET ME INTRODUCE YOU TO SHARI GRECO REICHES.
Wait, what's that? You already know her? You go way back with her?
You have friends in common? You've worked together? You know her
family? All of the above? As her business partner, I hear this all the time.

I've come to realize that Shari is connected to just about everyone.
Once, I was in the process of buying a house, and I mentioned the location to Shari. "Oh yeah, that's my mom's cousin's house, you'll like it,"
she told me. Of course she knew the house! You've heard of Six Degrees
of Kevin Bacon? It should be Six Degrees of Shari Greco Reiches ...

And everybody has a story about her. How she went the extra mile for
a friend during a tough time. How she guided a client through a difficult
change in life. How successful she was in leading one of her non-profit
boards. How hard she works. How thoughtful she is. It goes on ...

My story with Shari goes back to college. We met at the University
of Illinois in Champaign-Urbana, where we both studied accounting.
Over the years we kept in touch, and eventually found ourselves working as financial advisors in Sanford Bernstein's Chicago office. One day
I mentioned to her that a professional colleague we both knew might
be looking to start a private client advisory practice. What did she think
about going there with me?

Of course, she was one step ahead. She usually is. "Why do that
for him when we can do it for ourselves?" she asked. And, with that,
Rappaport Reiches Capital Management began.

It's been a great adventure, and we still have lots of chapters to write. And Shari's husband Stephen, who joined us during our first year in business, has been such a good friend and partner as well.

From day one her ideas, plans, and visions came furiously. A mile a minute. Or a minute a mile. We're used to sometimes having words mixed up a bit! But when Shari starts shaking her hands back and forth—just wait, something new is coming.

I have no idea where all that energy comes from. She is a force of nature. But her focus always begins and ends with doing the right thing for our clients.

Shari has a gift for taking complex concepts and bringing them to life so that they are understandable and relatable. I think she realized early on that I have a gift for the opposite ...

And that's what this book is about—taking financial planning and investing ideas that often can be complicated, and helping you use them to take control over the "money" part of your life.

You won't find the graphs and charts that adorn a typical financial planning book here. No mention of alpha or R-squared ratios (R-twos as Shari calls them) or anything like that. Just lots of common-sense ideas you can begin using today. And some pretty funny and heart-warming stories too.

Shari's approach works. I see its positive impact every day on our clients. It's the peace of mind they get from financial clarity and organization. The satisfaction of knowing their values are reflected in their financial decisions. The confidence they gain from following a thoughtful and disciplined plan.

If you know Shari, you know how much she cares about impacting as many lives as possible. Empowering people, especially women, to make smart decisions with their money is her life's mission. I think this book goes a long way towards accomplishing that.

And if you don't know her, you soon will. It's inevitable!

~David Rappaport

MY STORY

T O UNDERSTAND MY STORY, I need to start by telling you about my parents, Bess Greco Ekstein and Martin Bresloff.

My dad was an accountant and an entrepreneur, having started his own CPA firm at the age of 26 with his best friend, Gene Barasch.

While most of my girlfriends loved dolls and jewelry, I was fascinated with the electric tape machine calculator at his office. I would play with the number keys while he worked, adding numbers in my head and comparing the results with the adding machine.

A few years after starting the accounting firm, my father was diagnosed with embryonal cell carcinoma (Brian Piccolo disease) and passed away at the age of 32, leaving my mom with me (eight years old) and a newborn son, Adam.

As you can imagine, money was tight. My mom is a very strong person and found a way to make ends meet. She worked nights doing surveys and other jobs. My mom was a true role model, teaching me the value of working hard and forging ahead.

A few years later my mom was fixed up with Dante Greco. He was a banker and founded the Bank of Highwood in 1961 at age 33—at the time, the youngest person in the state of Illinois

Dad and me – so cute!

to start a bank. They married. It was her second fix-up and second marriage. Shortly after, Dante adopted Adam and me. Over the years he became my true mentor, my second dad, and the second entrepreneur in my life.

When I was 13, he started a second bank, the New Century Bank, in Mundelein, Illinois, and I accompanied him as he went door-to-door to offer stock to community members. So many doors closed quickly with a "no," but he never got discouraged. He would say, "It's okay to get the 'noes.' You need many, many 'noes' before you can get a 'yes.' So embrace the 'noes.'" My first sales lesson at age 14! Since then I have never been afraid of the noes.

During high school, I worked at the bank. My dad put me through all the departments—I started by filing checks, worked as a teller, and eventually processed loans and overdrafts. It was here I saw firsthand the stress money caused. There were overdrafts that could not be covered, loans that could not be approved. How did this happen? Why were so many people in trouble? At this point I knew I wanted to help people with their finances. Banking would be my calling.

When I attended University of Illinois, my dad gave me great career advice—study accounting. Understanding financial statements would make me a better banker and provide limitless possibilities.

I started at Arthur Andersen in Chicago, auditing banks. Shortly after, I met my husband Stephen. From day one he has been so supportive of my work. We are true life and work partners. We always split the responsibilities of raising our two wonderful daughters, Maddie and Isabel. The support of our friends, family and caregiver, Priscilla (for twelve years), enabled me to continue my career.

After a few years at Arthur Andersen, it was time for me to join my dad at the bank. I loved every minute working there—building relationships with clients, and helping them with loans and savings. I also learned to give back to my community.

Eight years flew by and the Board of Directors decided to sell the bank to First Colonial Bank. I was sad, but understood the decision.

And then the whirlwind started.

A few months later First Colonial was sold to Firstar, which was sold to Star Bank, which was sold to US Bank. Four mergers in three years!

After merger number one, I was promoted to President of the group of banks my dad started, and he was named President Emeritus. (Banks are big on titles …) By merger number four, I was President of Private Banking in Illinois. It was during this stint in private banking that I learned about investing, which quickly became a passion.

A few years after the bank sale, my dad passed away from leukemia. Banking was not the same without him. It was time to make a change. Stephen understood that I loved people, advising, and investing. He suggested I become a financial advisor. Smart guy!

This is where David Rappaport enters the picture. David and I were friends in college, both accounting majors, and he recruited me to his firm, Sanford Bernstein & Co. I began to build a successful financial advisory practice. Over time, I realized that I could best control my own destiny, as well as help guide my clients' destinies, by starting my own firm. David and decided to take the leap together. Rappaport Reiches Capital Management opened its doors in 2005. After our first year, Stephen left his law practice of twenty years and joined the fun.

So let me get back to my mom. My brother and sister-in-law fixed her up with Sam Ekstein. Her third fix-up, who became her third husband, Sam. (That's why we call her "the closer.") Sam is another entrepreneur and has been a big supporter of my family and me.

Hard work, a support system, entrepreneurship. You can see where I come from.

WHY I'VE WRITTEN THIS BOOK

EARLY ON, MY FAMILY EXPERIENCED financial stress, so I understand its impact. I saw my bank clients go through difficult times and have never forgotten their looks of sadness, even grief, at financial misfortune.

Fortunately, through my experience, I've learned there is a better way. It starts with educating yourself to make smart money decisions and proper financial planning.

I've always wanted to make a difference and financial education is financial empowerment.

I am a storyteller by nature. I am hoping my stories and exercises in the book will inspire you to make positive financial changes to Maximize Your Return on Life.

Let's get started!

~Shari Greco Reiches

INTRODUCTION

I T WAS SUNDAY NIGHT, AND I was planning for the week ahead. It was going to be a short and busy one at our wealth management firm, as my husband Stephen and I were leaving on Friday to visit his family in Washington, D.C. Stephen and I are both life partners and business partners, and with us sometimes it's hard to separate the two.

I had just finished a call with my daughter Maddie who was living in Kansas City, having started her first job out of college. She mentioned that she'd love to join us in D.C., but ... could we help out by paying for the plane ticket?

So we went online and saw that the price was $650 for a round-trip ticket! Normally, I would have agonized a bit and then said nope, too expensive, she'd have to join us next time. I'm known for saying "no" when it comes to spending, especially if I could have gotten something cheaper. However, today I decided to buy the ticket.

What changed? How was I able to make the decision so quickly?

I applied my own Maximizing Return on Life principles, a set of guidelines that I have developed, over time, while working with my financial planning clients.

Let me explain.

DETERMINING MY VALUES

As a financial advisor, I attend numerous conferences related to investing and financial planning. I have always had a special interest in educating and empowering women, so I was excited to attend a Women and

1

Wealth conference in Austin, Texas. The purpose was to network with other women financial advisors, share best practices, and gain insight into our own lives. I did not know at the time that this conference would be the catalyst for my Maximize Your Return on Life journey.

One of the sessions was about Core Values. These values, we were told, were those things that are most important in our lives—such as family, meaningful work, community, time, flexibility, education, and health.

I was skeptical. I felt like I knew my values and I was unsure what this session would teach me. We were told to dress comfortably, and that the "circle" would last several hours. No calls, texts, or emails. Would this be a waste of time?

There were 12 women seated in a circle. The lights were off and candles were scattered around the room. The session started with meditation to clear our minds. We were given a journal and asked to respond to a variety of questions. Thought-provoking questions, asking us who we really were and what we truly cared about. Not typical financial planning stuff.

With no distractions, everyone was engaged. Even though we had just met a few hours before, the conversations were deep. Looking at my answers, and discussing them with the group, I gained quite a bit more insight than I had expected—perhaps because I was at a time in my life where I had more perspective, maybe even some wisdom. My daughters were both in college and doing well. My business was growing and I had satisfaction helping our clients. I could take a breath and focus a little bit more on me.

Going through the exercises, I realized that I never had quite understood the significance of Core Values. I just assumed I knew my values, all of those things that were important to me. But Core Values are different. They are the most significant beliefs by which we strive to live.

Deeply held Core Values of mine rose to the surface, which explained some recent decisions I had made. For example, I had just taken on the role of chairing a major capital campaign for my synagogue. Given the added work, the late-night emails and the endless meetings, I had asked myself, "Why?" Others had asked as well! This session answered that for me. Community and philanthropy are Core Values in my life.

The conference led to further introspection. I started thinking about my profession, wealth management. Most advisors focus on maximizing return on investment: market predictions, stock picks, positioning the portfolio, the next opportunity …

Yet, something is missing. Our industry is so impressed with analytics and strategy that discussion of Core Values is often incidental.

My career has been based on helping clients meet their goals and objectives, offering the peace of mind that comes with a thoughtful financial plan. I understand their money situation inside and out, but I learn so much more! I know of their heartbreaks and struggles, the triumphs and challenges of their kids, the frustrations of their jobs, the highs and lows of their relationships, their hopes for the future.

I get to know what really matters to them. And while investment performance is important, it's rarely at the top of their minds.

How could I use these recent insights as I act as their trusted partner in financial decision making? I tried an experiment over the next few months. I flipped things around. Instead of starting our conversations with a review of recent investment performance, I began our discussion by asking clients about their Core Values.

I brought Core Values to the forefront.

The response was overwhelming. Many of them had never thought about their Core Values and how they tied into their financial and life plan. Many couples had never had a serious conversation about values. One couple laughed and said that they spent more time discussing the color of their new car than discussing their Core Values.

I have not regretted my decision to purchase that airline ticket for my daughter Maddie. We had a wonderful weekend with the family. Laughs, tears, and still more laughs. I had a smile on my face all weekend. It seemed like a small decision at the time, but that trip had a longer-term impact. Maddie's grandmother's health slipped months later. We can't take for granted the time we spend together as a family. Our time together reinforced the value of family that I hope to pass on to my children.

I now use my Core Values as a guide for decisions concerning my time and money. I often give myself permission to spend money based on my values, such as family (buying a plane ticket for my daughter to join the trip), while I strive to reduce spending on other things.

Using Core Values then became the foundation of a philosophy that developed over time: how to move beyond just maximizing return on investments and into Maximizing Return on Life.

MAXIMIZING YOUR RETURN …

We're going to start at the beginning, with your early and profound memories of money—memories that shape your relationship with money today. Then we'll move on to identifying your Core Values and using them as you make important decisions on how you spend your time and money.

We'll discuss effective financial planning and investing, as well as steps to ensure that your loved ones are protected. Teaching the next generation about smart money habits will provide peace of mind for everyone. And while you have their attention, share your Core Values with them. Over time, it is as important to pass these values on as it is to pass on your valuables.

Along the way, we'll remember all those things and people that we are grateful for, especially when times are tough.

Take some time thinking about the questions I ask. Explore your feelings and tap into your curiosity. If you don't know an answer right away, revisit the question later. There are no right or wrong answers. But there is a path forward to greater clarity.

UNDERSTANDING
Your Money Beliefs

EARLY MEMORIES OF MONEY

A s you begin the journey to Maximize Your Return on Life, I want you to think about one simple word:

MONEY

What are your beliefs and feelings about money?

Have you ever taken the time to think about how your relationship with money came about?

How do you feel inside when talking about spending, saving, and investing? Empowered? Nervous?

Really dig deep into your feelings about money and how they affect your financial decisions.

We form our beliefs about money at an early age. It is often the actions or messages passed down from our parents that guide us. These memories often influence, consciously or subconsciously, how we feel about money. They show up in the choices we make every day.

I have clients whose first experiences with money were difficult. Decisions they make today are influenced by challenging times years ago. Some clients grew up during the Great Depression, with their relationship to money forged during a time of scarcity. Today, we have young people whose first experiences with money came about during the Great Recession of 2008-2009.

Other clients have very positive early memories of money, even if their family was not particularly financially well-off. I often hear clients say, "I guess I grew up in a poor household, only we didn't know it at the time!"

Here are some of their stories:

JOE's parents were very status-conscious and always owned fancy cars and an impressive house. Later in life, Joe's father lost his job. The family had to downsize their lifestyle almost overnight. Joe remembers his father at the kitchen table, sorting through bills with a worried look on his face. While Joe is doing well as a professional now, he still fears that his financial security can be taken away at any time. He is anxious when paying bills.

JANE's parents handed her money whenever she asked, and sometimes even when she didn't ask. Her parents never encouraged her to find a meaningful career path and thought that her happiness was tied to having anything she wanted. As an adult, she relies too often on others to provide for her.

ANITA remembers her mom walking into a store and heading straight for the sale rack. If it wasn't on sale, she didn't buy it. Anita has trouble today buying anything that isn't marked down and isn't sure that's always the best approach.

NIA had to earn her allowance by doing chores. Her parents encouraged her to save a portion for a "big" item and donate a portion to her church. She feels today that by learning these habits she has developed a positive relationship with money.

EVAN remembered running a lemonade stand during Northwestern football games. His parents provided the capital (lemonade, cups, a pitcher, etc.) and he kept the profits. Early on, he learned the joy of providing a service that people valued. He saved his lemonade money and bought a cherished scooter. As an adult, he worked at several large companies, but finally decided to start his own business. He now is happier than ever and has the same feeling he had at the lemonade stand.

DANIEL's father was a lawyer who worked all the time. Most days his father left before he was awake and came home after he was asleep. His father missed most of his sports events and never really seemed to be present. Daniel decided at an early age he would have a career that offered more flexibility and family time. The big house just wasn't as important, and he feels good about this choice.

It takes some time to look back at your early memories of money: your first bank account, birthday money gifts, and your first job. Your earliest memories of money may be your most profound—those that have a lasting impact on your life.

So, what are your most meaningful early memories of money?

It's an intriguing question, right? If you can't come up with a memory right away, keep thinking. Once you have your memory, see if there are any parallels to your current feelings about money.

Here are some questions to help you get started:

QUESTIONS

How did your parents handle money?

Did they spend or save?

Did they try to influence your habits?

Did they talk about money? Fight about it?

Was money a taboo topic for family discussions?

Were you a saver or a spender as a child?

What was your first job?

How did it make you feel to earn your own money? What did you do with it?

Does one of your memories shape your money behaviors today?

Do any of your money beliefs cause stress in relationships with loved ones?

Are there any changes in your money beliefs that you would like to make, now that you have thought more about your early or most profound memories of money?

Discuss these questions with your loved ones. Identifying what has impacted your early relationship with money gives you the power to make changes in your life today.

BABYSITTING AND BANKING

I'm so lucky to have very favorable early memories of money.

As a young teenager, most Saturday nights I babysat kids in my neighborhood. On grid-lined paper, I charted my earnings, hour by hour (don't worry ...I still kept an eye on the kids). As each hour passed, I added to the bar representing my pay.

Many of my friends took their hard-earned babysitting money and bought jewelry and clothes, but not me. I was a banker's daughter and my earnings went straight into my savings account. My dad, Dante Greco, founded the Bank of Highwood in Illinois. He always preached that we should pay ourselves first by saving before spending.

I have fond memories of my visits to the bank. With my treasured savings passbook in one hand and dollar bills in the other, I would wait in the teller line (no cutting in front just because I was the boss's kid!). When I reached the front, I made my deposit with such a smile!

I can still hear the *clickety-clack* of the teller's machine recording my deposit in the book. I knew the importance of compound interest (banks paid 5% in those days!) and loved to watch my balance go up line by line. Today, when I check my account balances online, I still listen for that *clickety-clack*, instinctively telling me that I'm doing ok. I wish they could add that sound to the app on my phone ...

I loved to visit my dad in his office. He had a bowl of candy for customers and I considered myself a good one. Okay, there were some perks to being the boss's kid! I knew everyone—the local business owners who needed loans, the workers who would cash their paychecks, the tellers and bank staff. It really was a community bank. I miss those days. I can still smell the coffee and donuts on Fridays and Saturdays.

When I turned 16, I was so excited that in addition to babysitting, I could find other jobs. Even then I was competitive, so I found three. I worked at a country club, a pizzeria, and a frozen yogurt store.

Those paychecks meant everything to me. It was more than the money—those paychecks gave me a sense of freedom and independence. In the back of my mind I started to realize that I wanted to control my own destiny and working hard could get me there.

My parents were very supportive. One evening my dad came into the yogurt store to take me home, and he actually swept the floor so I could leave sooner. My mom always waited for me to come home from the pizza parlor and together we'd eat my free pizza.

One day, my dad suggested I buy Bank of Highwood stock with my savings. I was too young to counter, "Dad, stock tips rarely pay off. I would be better off in a broadly diversified global stock portfolio," so I purchased ten shares. The stock never paid a dividend, but in 1994, we sold the bank and those shares became very valuable. The proceeds helped me with the down payment on my first home.

**I treasured the time working
with my dad at the bank.**

My first money lesson was the power of saving and compounding returns over time. But it was even more than that; it also was the pride of a job—or two or three.

TAKEAWAYS

It's helpful to look back on your childhood memories about money.

Those early or profound experiences shape your beliefs and the decisions you make about money today.

This knowledge can give you the power to make positive changes in your current relationship with money.

Your beliefs about money may impact how your loved ones, especially children, develop their own relationships with money.

IDENTIFYING
Your Core Values

YOUR LIFE'S GROCERY LIST

Have you ever gone to the grocery store without a list? We all know what happens next. You spend extra time going through all the aisles. Your mind is racing: *What do I need? Do we have ketchup at home? How about eggs?* You are a little hungry, so chocolate-covered banana snacks and a bag of weird wasabi-flavored chips end up in the cart.

As you stand in the checkout line, you start thinking: *Wasn't there something I actually came here for?* By now you've forgotten, which means once you return home your spouse is going to "request" you go right back and get the laundry detergent. Now!

The trip would have been more productive if you had taken just a bit of time upfront to make a list. But you didn't, so you spent money on things you didn't need and wasted time meandering through the aisles. You were less confident in deciding what to buy, weren't you? Next time, bring your list.

As we face decisions on family, careers, lifestyles, philanthropy—how we spend our time and money—we could use a similar list to keep us on track and point us in the right direction. A list of what's truly important to us, a list that can provide guidance as we navigate our way through life. The items on that list—those are your Core Values.

Which Core Values fill your cart?

While a grocery list may take a few minutes, your list of Core Values may take a little more time. Let's get started.

What Are Core Values?

Core Values are the priorities that you value most in your life—such as family, meaningful work, or giving back to your community. Perhaps health and fitness, or the flexibility to come and go as you please.

Core Values are not possessions, activities, or experiences. They are aspects of **how you define yourself as a person. They bring about the most positive impact on your life.**

They exist on the highest plane. For example, love of music is not a core value. But if part of you yearns to express yourself creatively—well, that is where you start. Creativity and expression are the Values, music is the medium, and piano lessons may be the means.

Core Values act as a guide to help give you clarity in major decisions in your life. They can help you set goals and priorities. At the very least, they are your grocery list for life!

So How Do You Determine Your Core Values?

The following questions will get you thinking:

What brings energy to your life?

What do you strive to accomplish over time?

What achievements are you most proud of?

What areas within your life do you protect the most?

Where are you willing to make the fewest compromises?

What qualities do the people you admire possess?

What is the legacy you would like to leave?

Considering the questions above, look at the list below and circle any of the words that you feel could be a Core Value. Don't think too hard—just circle. If you don't see one that captures your thinking, add it to the list and circle it.

Authenticity	Achievement	Adventure
Authority	Autonomy	Balance
Beauty	Boldness	Compassion
Challenge	Community	Competency
Competition	Contribution	Creativity
Curiosity	Determination	Fairness
Faith	Fame	Family
Friendships	Flexibility	Fun
Growth	Happiness	Health
Honesty	Humor	Influence
Inner Harmony	Justice	Kindness
Knowledge	Leadership	Legacy
Love	Loyalty	Meaningful Work
Optimism	Peace	Philanthropy
Pleasure	Poise	Power
Popularity	Recognition	Religion
Reputation	Respect	Responsibility
Security	Self-Respect	Service
Spirituality	Stability	Success
Status	Trustworthiness	Wealth

Spend some time looking at the words you circled,
take a breath and narrow the list to your top twenty values.

Now narrow it to the top ten.

Take some time and now narrow it to five.
Okay, overachievers, you can have up to ten if you need to!

Once you have your Core Values list, write it down here:

1. _____

2. _____

3. _____

4. _____

5. _____

Other Values: _____

_____

_____

Keep this list handy. We're going to refer back to it as we move forward
and look at decisions about how you spend your time and money.

Share your Values

Once you determine your Core Values, don't keep them to yourself! Share them with your life partner, your best friend, your kids, or anyone important to you. Talk about why you feel certain values better reflect who you are, and why others may not. Talk about how your values impact your decisions in life.

QUESTIONS

Were there any surprises in discovering your Core Values?

Have you used your Core Values in making any big decisions in your life?

- Which decisions?

- What Core Values guided you?

MY CORE VALUE—FAMILY

It was easy for me to find the first value to circle: Family.

I immediately thought back to when our kids were young and we visited my parents and extended family in Florida during winter break. As we started the long drive, I hoped our girls were filled with excitement and anticipation, but they weren't. Nope. We just got a few big sighs ... To add spice, I mapped out the drive with educational and food stops: Elvis's home, Ruby Falls, and Coke Factory in Atlanta, to name a few.

On occasion, like every year, the kids asked if we could try something different. How about the hot new resort in Mexico? I always explained to the kids that these were special times we could all spend together in Florida. The grandparents, the cousins, all of us.

As the kids got older, they began to understand. We made a lifetime of memories: all the cousins sleeping on blow-up mattresses, making dinner for 20+, bingo nights, swimming at the pool, long walks, and quality time with the grandparents.

My family thinking about fun on the beach.
I'm wondering if we have enough sunscreen.

Core Values Change Over Time

As your life changes, your Core Values will as well.

Liam had "Status" as a Core Value. He felt he grew up on the wrong side of town and as a kid, was embarrassed to have friends over. So, as his career progressed, he had the chance to buy a showcase house. But as he got older, his perspective changed. The showcase house meant showcase expenses, and he no longer cared about impressing anyone. He had moved on, and now placed a greater Value on life flexibility: not being tied down by maintenance and costs. He downsized and was much happier.

Ingrid valued "Achievement" when she was in her 30s. She worked hard to build her career while raising three children. She became managing partner in her firm. Once her youngest went to college, she spent some time thinking about her own college years. Memories of trips she made, often to exotic places. On her own! The stories she could tell! Back then, she valued "Adventure," but eventually put that on the back burner. Now that her career was in a good place, she decided to book adventure trips: hiking in Peru, whitewater rafting in Costa Rica. Her prior Value had resurfaced, and she followed it.

TAKEAWAYS

Incorporating your Core Values into your decisions can prevent you from wasting precious time and money, and from getting sidetracked or confused as to your next move. An added bonus—you will feel more confident in your decisions!

Your Core Values may also permit you to explore choices that in the past you may have dismissed.

Share your Core Values with your loved ones.

Core Values can change over time.

MAXIMIZE
the Return of Your Spending

THE BIG PURCHASE:
SHOULD YOU FEEL GUILTY OR NOT GUILTY?

C lients often tell me they feel they are being judged on what they spend. They feel like they need to support their case when making a large purchase. And, they often feel guilty afterwards.

Hmm … Judging … cases … guilt …? Sounds like an episode of a courtroom TV show! Let's watch …

ℒ ℒ ℒ

WELCOME TO
"THE BIG PURCHASE:
SHOULD YOU FEEL GUILTY OR NOT GUILTY?"
STARRING JUDGE SHARI REICHES.

TODAY'S EPISODE:
"The Case of the Awesome Bike"

THE PURCHASER:
Stephen Reiches, husband of Shari Reiches

THE ITEM:
An awesome all-carbon gravel bike

THE QUESTION:
Should Stephen feel …Guilty or Not Guilty?
Let's enter the courtroom.

ℒ ℒ ℒ

BAILIFF:
All rise for Judge Shari.

JUDGE SHARI:
You may be seated. Mr. Reiches, today, we are here to decide whether your recent purchase of a bicycle should cause you to feel guilty or not guilty. May I see the evidence?

STEPHEN:
Really, Shari?

JUDGE SHARI (SLAMMING GAVEL):
You will refer to me as Judge Shari.

STEPHEN:
Yes ma'am. I mean yes, Judge. It's awesome! One hundred percent carbon, disc brakes and Di2 shifters. (Hands picture of bike to bailiff, who gives to Judge Shari.)

JUDGE SHARI:
What about the receipt?

STEPHEN:
Here, your honor. It was a steal at $2,500. It normally sells for …

JUDGE SHARI:
Enough. I get it. How did you decide it was okay to buy a new bike?

STEPHEN:
Well, for starters, my cycling buddies told me there is a formula for the optimal number of bikes to own.

JUDGE SHARI:
I can't wait to hear it …

STEPHEN:
The optimal number of bikes is $x + 1$,
where x = my current number of bikes.

JUDGE SHARI:

Really, Stephen? If that is your defense, I am about to declare a guilty verdict, but I am going to give you one last chance, because, it is … an awesome bike. There are three things to consider when making purchases like this.

First, do you set a budget for spending?

STEPHEN:

Yes, I do. At the beginning of each year, I start by projecting my after-tax income. I take this amount and set up a budget, including savings and discretionary spending.

JUDGE SHARI:

Budgeting! That's Step One. So far so good.
How do you know you are following your budget?

STEPHEN:

Well, it's a little bit of work, but I download all of our monthly spending into a spreadsheet and make sure everything gets put in the correct categories. I can quickly see if the family is over or under budget either monthly or on an annual basis.
And so far, we are right on track.
The bike purchase fits in the "health and fitness" budget category.

JUDGE SHARI:

Tracking! Excellent. That's Step Two. But there's one more consideration when we look at spending. Step Three is …
aligning your spending with your—

STEPHEN (INTERRUPTING):

My Core Values! I'm a big fan of your blog, Judge Shari.
I just read about Core Values in *Your Life's Grocery List.*
Excellent writing, by the way.

JUDGE SHARI:

I agree.

STEPHEN:

I do try to align my spending with my values. Health, fitness, and adventure are high on my list. Riding helps me achieve my fitness goals. Plus, it gives my lovely wife some alone time in the morning to achieve that Core Value of inner harmony. Win, Win!

JUDGE SHARI:

Spare me. I have never mentioned inner harmony in my life.
But I do have a verdict in the Case of the Awesome Bike.
My decision as to whether you should feel Guilty or Not Guilty is …

**Tune in next week for Judge Shari's verdict.
How do you think she will rule? How would you?**

GUILTY
or
Not Guilty?

CREATING YOUR BUDGET:
THE 50/20/30 RULE

J udge Shari and defendant Stephen referred to a spending budget. How do you create one?

There's a simple solution.

Start with your after-tax income. That's your salary, reduced by the amount withheld for federal taxes, state taxes, and payroll taxes. Of this amount, you should budget approximately 50% to your needs, 20% to saving & debt reduction, and 30% to your wants.

Let's take a look at each of these.

50%: Needs

These items are your essentials, your basic needs. There is not much you can do to change these numbers, unless you are willing to make major lifestyle changes. We'll talk about that in a bit.

- Groceries

- Housing
    - Mortgage or rent
    - Real estate taxes
    - Homeowners insurance
    - Repairs and maintenance

- Basic utilities

- Health insurance (if not already deducted from paycheck)

- Medical expenses

- Other insurance: life, disability, auto, etc.

- Transportation
    - Car payments
    - Gas, repairs and maintenance
    - Public transportation, Uber rides, etc.

- Minimum loan payments

- Childcare and other expenses allowing you to work

- Alimony, maintenance, child support

20%: Debt repayment and Savings

- Reduce debt
  - Credit card balances
  - Student loan payments
  - Other personal loans
- Build your emergency/rainy day fund
  - 3 to 6 months of "needs" spending in a savings account
- Retirement plans – 401 (k) plans, IRAs etc.
- Savings for large purchases
  - Future home down payment
  - Car
  - Other major planned purchases
- College savings
- Additional investment savings

30%: Wants

These are discretionary items, and you have more flexibility here.

- Dining out/entertainment
- Travel
- Luxury purchases (jewelry, art …)
- Hobby spending
- Gym memberships

Implementing the 50/20/30 Rule

Your after-tax income is the foundation of your budget.

Now take the time to track where your after-tax income goes. Try to use a reasonably long period of time, at least six months. From your morning Starbucks to your electric bill, it all counts. You can use an online app, personal finance software, an excel spreadsheet, or plain old pencil and paper.

After that is done, put each expense in one of the 50/20/30 categories and calculate the percentages for each category.

FILL IN YOUR PERCENTAGES

Needs: _____

Debt repayment and savings: _____

Wants: _____

Do your spending decisions line up with the 50/20/30 guidelines?

Any surprises?

Do you have a method to keep track of your budget and keep you accountable?

What changes in your spending do you plan to make?

YOUR SPENDING, YOUR CORE VALUES

The budgeting process is all about choices. How do you make these spending decisions? Use your Core Values as a guide.

Spending on Needs:

Your Needs spending percentage is difficult to reduce in the short-run. Much of Needs spending is based on longer-term commitments that you have already made, such as buying a house.

Is your Needs percentage higher than 50%?

It could be that you chose to live in a more expensive area to be in a certain school district. Or you may have chosen to live closer to work so you can spend more time with your family. These decisions are based on your Core Values, and the trade-off is that you may have to reduce your Wants expenses.

Is your Needs percentage below 50%?

You may have the flexibility to save more or spend more on your Wants.

If you are retired and have paid off your mortgage, your Needs percentage may be well below 50%. You are fortunate that you can allocate more to the other categories—saving money in a college 529 savings plan for a loved one, spending more money on your Wants. You deserve it.

Savings/Debt Repayment:

A question I often get is, should I pay off my debt first, or save towards retirement in my employer's retirement plan? If your debt is overwhelming your budget and you are paying high interest rates, start there. If the debt is manageable, try to do both—save a portion of each paycheck for retirement and continue to pay down debt.

When you have reached that terrific moment of getting rid of debt, take a moment and celebrate. Once the celebration is over, take that monthly payment you used to make and allocate those funds towards savings.

Spending on Wants:

This is the fun area! You have complete discretion here, but you want to use these dollars wisely. Do you love to wear designer clothes, enjoy sporting events, theater or travel? The choice is yours. You should decide what will bring you joy.

Once again, look to your Core Values to help decide on spending on your wants.

List the top 5 expenses in this category
and match the expense with one of your Core Values:

1. Expense_____

   Core Value _____

2. Expense_____

   Core Value _____

3. Expense_____

   Core Value _____

4. Expense_____

   Core Value _____

5. Expense_____

   Core Value _____

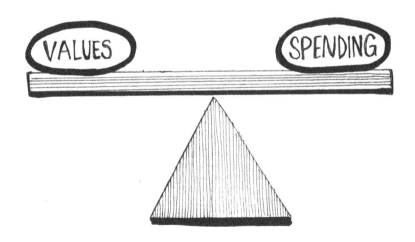

QUESTIONS

When it comes to your spending:

Do your major expenses align with your Core Values?

Are there expenses that do not align with your Core Values?

Do you have a Core Value that is not represented on this spending list?

Did you have an "Aha!" moment?

Here are some examples of clients who used their **Core Values** to make spending decisions:

BEN AND GITA worked more than 50 hours a week and owned two homes and expensive cars. Through these discussions, they realized that they missed the freedom they had when they were younger. They felt tied down by their jobs and possessions. So, we worked together to come up with a five-year plan to simplify their lives.

James had never had a nice car. He always admired cars and dreamed of owning a Corvette one day. He worked hard. He saved money when he could. He decided that he really wanted this car. To him it was a sign of his hard work, a goal he had always had, and he felt great every time he drove the car.

Crystal realized that her Values called for finding significant meaning in her work. She had been at the same job for several years, and though it was enjoyable, it was not fulfilling. Could she transition to working at a beloved nonprofit organization at a lower salary? We worked on her budget and she began a job search. It was a trade-off, but by paring certain expenses, this value could be achieved. An added benefit—I have never seen her more energized and excited!

Jasmine lived in New York and wanted to help her daughter Molly, who just had a baby and was living in California. But Jasmine always had been very frugal and was even willing to sleep on Molly's couch. I suggested she rent an apartment, but Jasmine was hesitant. Once we quantified the cost and added it as a new line item in her financial plan, she realized she could afford it. Mom, daughter, and especially son-in-law were thrilled. Jasmine recently emailed a picture of all of them together and there were smiles from ear to ear.

All values decisions are not epic. Using your Core Values as a guide is helpful even for smaller spending decisions:

You love to cook but don't have time to prepare for the meal. Should you buy the pre-chopped onions? You know you are paying three times as much, but if you value your free time it's money well-spent. No tears on that decision!

The train is running late and you are meeting a cherished friend. Should you wait for the bus or pay a little extra and take a cab or car service? Will hopping in the cab maximize the time spent with a friend?

You are having a dinner party. Should you pay for some help in the kitchen? You spend so much time and energy getting the food ready. Would having help make the night more enjoyable?

Once you align your spending with your Core Values, you will have more confidence, less stress, and less guilt surrounding your spending decisions. Whether you spend a large or small amount of money, you feel more fulfilled and in control when your expenditures are aligned with your Values.

WHAT IS THE KEY TO FINANCIAL HAPPINESS?

- Living within your means. Spending less than you have coming in.

- Do this and everything else will fall into place.

- Live beyond your means and you will face stress and anxiety. Your flexibility to make life and career decisions will be limited. Your relationships will be negatively impacted.

- If you find that you are living beyond your means, you have the power to change. It starts with using your Core Values as a guide to budgeting and spending.

By applying these principles, you will have the key to financial happiness.

The Key to Financial Success

MY MONEY MULTIPLIERS

For years I have reviewed my own budget and clients' budgets and have kept a list of ways to save money.

I call these tips Money Multipliers. Start with the non-negotiables. These are the must-dos.

Non-Negotiable Tips

1. Pay off your credit card in full every month.

2. Establish automatic payment for your bills to avoid late fees.

3. Banking accounts:

   - Know the minimum balance needed to avoid monthly maintenance fees.

   - Set up overdraft protection—avoid overdrafts and their related fees.

   - Check on interest rates for accounts. Do you have too much money in a checking account paying 0%? Move some to an interest-bearing savings account.

   - Use your bank's ATM network. Those $3 out-of-network fees can add up.

4. Insurance:

- Compare insurance prices: Auto, Home, Life, Disability, and Long-Term Care.

- Know your health insurance plans and options.

5. Home expenses:

- Review your real estate taxes. If they seem high relative to other homes in your area, appeal them.

- Check your mortgage rate vs. current rates. You may find significant savings by refinancing.

- Maintain your home diligently to avoid, or at least defer, big ticket items in the future.

6. Understand your employee benefits.

- Contribute at least as much to your 401(k) plan as needed to get the match offered by your employer.

- Know all your benefits and review them on an annual basis.

- Take advantage of company discounts.

7. Check your credit report annually.

A few extra tips that add up.

1. Reduce your dining out expense: eat at home, bring your lunch.

2. Keep a list when shopping to avoid impulse buys.

3. Reduce your home expenses.

   - Weatherproof your home.

   - Use LED bulbs.

   - Use an automatic thermostat.

4. Transportation

   - Keep maintenance on your car up to date.

   - Drive your car an extra year or two.

   - Evaluate whether you really need an extra car.

   - Use public transportation when possible.

   - Use apps for parking like Spot Hero.

   - Know where you can get low gas prices and keep your tank half full.

   - Carpool.

5. Travel

   - Compare several websites for hotels, airfare, trips, and entertainment.

   - Buy your tickets early and travel during nonpeak times when practical.

6. Cancel subscriptions you are not using: health clubs, magazines, newspapers, diet, and food services to name a few.

7. Gift cards: know where they are and use them. They lose value over time.

8. Carry a water bottle. Save the environment and reduce your bottled water expense.

9. Rethink expensive drinks. Fancy coffee and fancy cocktails add up over time.

10. Buy in bulk.

11. Invest in reusable bags, lunch boxes, and other containers.

12. Prescriptions: price compare generic, bulk, 90-day supplies.

13. Borrow or rent large-ticket items, including clothes.

14. Evaluate your technology needs: cable, phones, and computers.

15. Use a library card instead of buying books.

16. Use one in/one out concept—if you buy something, get rid of something.

TAKEAWAYS

There are two items to consider when making a purchase:

- Does the purchase fit within your budget?

- Does your spending align with your Core Values?

Spend your money on what you value most and reduce spending money on what you don't value.

Establish a budget and track your expenses.

Whether you spend a large or small amount of money, you will feel more fulfilled and in control when your expenditures are aligned with your Values.

MAXIMIZE
Your Return on Time

IS YOUR TIME BUDGET OVERDRAWN?

Creating a budget aligned with your Values (and sticking to it) can take the stress and guilt out of spending decisions. The same concept applies to decisions on how you spend your time. There are a finite number of hours in a day. Time is a very valuable currency and should be used wisely.

This is a lesson I recently learned. Every month I review my finances. I reconcile my bank account and look at my expenses versus my budget. I have been doing this for years.

But my calendar … that's another story. Calendar invites fill my in-box, and I hit accept. Invites for work meetings, social events, and my non-profit board activities. No screening process. If I'm available, I accept. Don't get me wrong, I enjoy being busy, but I never really looked at my time until my daughter Isabel tore her ACL while skiing, during her junior year at the University of Denver.

If I say 'yes' to all of these, what will I have to say 'no' to?

Isabel has a great sense of humor. She posted a picture on Instagram of her being taken off the mountain on a ski patrol sled. Her caption—"**Go big or go home.**"

She went big *and* she went home! Isabel had surgery in Chicago during her spring break. The day before she was to return to school, we all realized she was going to need some help.

I quickly booked a trip to Denver for the week to help get her situated. No problem, how hard could it be to leave for a week? I opened my calendar and was surprised at all the activity. Where did all this stuff come from? There were client meetings, management meetings, date night, social events, an industry dinner, networking events, Cubs tickets, a birthday dinner, and caring for my neighbor's cat (don't worry—my husband Stephen took care of Fuzzy).

Wow. What a busy week. Maybe this was an unusual one. I looked at the week before and the week after. I was booked solid those weeks too. Obviously, it had been a while since I took a long look at how my time was allocated. My head started spinning. I took a deep look at my calendar and some themes started to emerge. Did I really say "yes" to all these commitments? I needed to be more intentional with my time.

While reviewing my calendar, I asked myself an important question:

- Is how I am spending my time aligned with my Core Values?

From this exercise, I realized the following:

- I was not spending enough time on one of my Core Values: health. I needed more time to make healthy meals and go to the gym. I decided to schedule my workouts like I schedule work appointments.

- I needed to be more selective about the business networking events I attended.

- I should not automatically accept calendar meeting invites. Did I really need to attend that event, meeting, or lunch?

- Although "Giving Back" is a Core Value of mine, I was participating in too many non-profit boards and seemed to be stretched a little thin. Late night meetings interfered with early morning workouts. When my next board terms are over, I will not automatically renew. I will think through all the options.

I tend to be a "yes" person. Now that I have learned to understand the consequences of always saying "yes," what will I have to say "no" to as a result?

Each hour is important. Budget your time wisely.

QUESTIONS

How are you currently spending your time?

Does your time align with your values?

Do you enjoy all these activities?

Any changes you would like to make?

OF CLUTTER, I UTTER

I have been hearing people talk about clutter for years. Clutter is everywhere in our lives.

Clutter is a time destroyer. We are constantly spending time looking for important documents, car keys, shoes, etc. All this extra time adds up. It's exhausting. A major time waster.

Clutter can be costly in other ways too

Increases Stress

Clutter has been known to increase stress levels. It can overload your senses. Stuff everywhere can be unsettling. Clutter in the home is a constant reminder of work to be done.

Clutter Costs Money

Have you paid late fees because a bill was hidden under a pile of papers? Have you bought things that you already own, but couldn't find?

These costs may seem nominal, but they add up ... and add additional clutter. Here are some observations about clutter from friends and colleagues:

ANDREW mentioned that his garage was so full, he had to park his car outside and it was vandalized.

MARIA added that she loves the feeling of dropping boxes off at Goodwill—it brings a sigh of relief that she is getting organized while helping others at the same time.

GRACE said that when she moved two years ago, she never unpacked ten boxes and they were still in her basement. They probably will stay there until her next move. Did she really need to keep all that junk and pay to move it?

SOFIA's mother recently moved into an assisted living facility. The responsibility for getting Mom's home ready for sale fell to her. Her mother never threw anything away and my friend had to sort through 50 years of collected items. (The actual words my friend used to describe the clutter cannot be printed.) The effort took over her weekends for months, taking her away from family, and led to resentment between the two of them. My friend vowed that she would never make her children go through the same experience.

THE CLUTTER QUIZ

Here's a quiz to see how clutter affects your life: **Give yourself one point for each yes—and be honest!**

[ ] Have you ever bought something you already owned because you couldn't find the original item?

[ ] Do you spend several minutes each day looking for something? (Yes, this includes your keys and phone.)

[ ] Do you have a junk drawer in your kitchen that is completely full? (One point for each full drawer.)

[ ] Do you own extra towels, blankets, and sheets that don't match because "someone will want them someday?"

[ ] Do you have expired medications? (Can you find your medications?)

[ ] Do you own old appliances you never use, such as a bread machine or a frozen margarita maker that you were going to use over the summer?

[ ] Do you have a pile of mail, magazines, catalogs, or newspapers that you are "eventually going to get through?"

☐ Do you have trouble figuring out what to wear even though your closet is full of clothes? (Give yourself two points if you have clothes in closets that you have forgotten about!)

☐ Do you rent a storage unit?

☐ Is your refrigerator full of cartons of the same stuff, all with different expiration dates?

☐ Do you park your car outside since you can't fit it in the garage?

☐ Do things fall out of your cupboards when you open them?

☐ Do you have more than 100 unopened messages in your email inbox?

☐ Do you have a coffee mug for each day of the month? (Give yourself two points if they all have witty sayings.)

☐ Do you own unused gift cards that have expired? (Give yourself an extra point if you think you have unused cards, but can't find them.)

☐ Have you been late in paying bills because you misplaced them?

☐ Have you ever discovered that something you loved was ruined because it wasn't stored properly?

☐ Does clutter cause you stress?

Sum up your score. Here are my thoughts on your total:

0 POINTS
We will cover lying and its harmful effects
on relationships in the future.

1-2 POINTS
You could write this chapter!
Please come to my house and help me get organized.

3-5 POINTS
You are on your way,
but still could use some strategies to declutter.

6-19 POINTS
I'm here to help! Please keep reading.

20+ POINTS
Reality TV is looking for you.

No congratulations for a high score, but trust me, you are not alone. In addition to costing us time, money and productivity, clutter causes unnecessary stress.

Let's Begin the Process

You can buy the Marie Kondo book or watch her show. My approach is much simpler!

Where to begin? Your calendar.

Schedule a time to declutter, just like other things on your to-do list. Pick a quiet Sunday afternoon and I suggest starting with some music. Barry Manilow, Taylor Swift, Drake ... (well, that's what I would put on.)

Start with one room at a time. Pretend you are moving—so everything needs to come out of the closets, drawers, and shelves. Literally everything. Empty the room. Furniture too. I bet you don't put all of the furniture back—finally time to get rid of Aunt Millie's ottoman.

Divide your stuff into four categories:

1. THROW OUT

2. KEEP

3. DONATE

4. STORE FOR LATER

Next step: Throw out everything you are storing for later. Just kidding. Well, not really.

Less is more! Get rid of:

- Your unused pasta maker. You are not going to have a dinner party with friends gushing over your hand-made rigatoni.

- Clothes that you never wear but have sentimental value. Take a picture.

- Clothes that never fit properly. Sorry, girlfriends.

- Stephen, if you're reading this—throw out your ratty 1997 Cleveland Indians jersey. We all know what happened in Game 7.

- Your kid's third-grade art projects. Give them back to your kids with love! Okay, maybe keep one for sentimental value.

- Your old cross-country skis. Yeah, right, you'll start up again next year ...

- Your gardening tools. You live in a condo.

Find a convenient place for everything that's left. Finish one room before moving on to the next. And keep an eye out for future clutter. Stop it before it starts! Before you buy anything, shop your home first. Do you really need it?

Keep what is meaningful and what truly can't be replaced. The decision-making process—what stays and what goes—can be cathartic.

Once you have spent the time to declutter, relax, and take time to enjoy your more spacious home (where did you put that wine glass?), I promise you'll want to keep things that way.

DELETE DIGITAL CLUTTER

Now that you have eliminated your physical clutter you must be feeling very good. However, there is another type of clutter that might be causing you stress: Digital Clutter.

In our quest to be more productive, we store so much information on our computers, tablets, and smartphones. This can be overwhelming. Scrolling through emails, photos, and unused apps can make it hard to focus. Sound familiar?

Technology certainly has been helpful to our lives. However, it's time to take more control. Here are some suggestions to reduce digital clutter:

Your Inbox

What if you opened your mailbox and there were letters from six months ago still in the box? You remove the mail from your physical mailbox every day, but what about your electronic mailbox? How many old items do you have? Have you looked at the same email every day for the last two months? Every email takes time to read and process, and doing it over and over again adds up to many hours of time. Here are some tips to clean up your inbox:

- Delete emails you no longer need, especially emails over 30 days old.

- Find dedicated time to check your email—not every five minutes.

- Respond to emails that take less than a few minutes to reply. Flag emails that will take some time to respond, or move them to a separate file folder.

- Unsubscribe from (or send to the Spam folder) junk emails that you do not wish to receive.

Desktop/Laptop

When you open your computer do you have a lot of items taking up the virtual desktop? It is the equivalent of working on a cluttered desk. Just keep the icons you use most often. Get rid of icons you never use.

Smartphone

Extra apps, pictures, music, and notes are all taking up space on your phone. Once a month, go through all these items and delete the ones you are not using.

Photos

Your precious photos should be stored on the Cloud. What would you do if you damaged or lost your phone? Make digital albums with your favorite photos. Delete photos that serve no purpose (the picture of your parking space or an item you wanted to purchase). Do this at least once a month.

Facebook/Twitter/Instagram/games

You have over 1,000 Facebook friends and even more on Instagram. Congratulations! I know it is fun and you enjoy keeping up with everyone. However, this is time-consuming. Pick up the phone and call a friend. Meet her for coffee. Share pictures in person. You won't regret it.

Candy Crush, and other games, can be addicting. Do you really need to reach your all-time high score?

Password/Log-Ins

All these passwords! Trying to remember them can be frustrating. Especially when sites make you change them all the time. It is helpful to use a password app (which I will talk about in a bit).

Purge all the digital devices you no longer use (cameras, thumb drives, cell phone, hard drives)

Chances are your home is filled with these devices. If you do not need them all, try to donate them. If you can't, then recycle them properly. There are often special recycling days in your town for this equipment.

Deleting digital clutter will make you more efficient and save time each day.

QUESTIONS

What steps will you take to delete digital clutter?

Does adapting the latest technology free up time for you or add to your list of things to do?

ZAP YOUR ENERGY ZAPPER!

Clutter is a good example of an energy zapper—something that puts a frown on your face and instantly changes your mood, and not for the better. The good news—these annoying inconveniences usually can be fixed with a little bit of work.

My big zapper is keeping track of all my passwords. Uggghh!

I love how technology, especially my phone apps, make many of my daily activities (banking, shopping, even parking) easier. Until I bought a new phone and needed to re-input all my passwords. A time-consuming task fraught with peril!

My first clue that it did not go well happened on my way out of the Apple store. I went to Starbucks and my trusted app did not work. (Hey, a latte every now and then is still okay.) I had to sign in. What was the password? No idea. The Energy Zapping begins!

Luckily, I have a brother who works in tech. If you don't, I recommend you get one! He told me about an app that creates complex passwords and saves them in all one place. More security and less stress.

The app required a small fee and dedicated time to set up all my accounts with a new, secured password. About four hours, to be exact. But now that it's done, no more energy being zapped! And I feel the power every time I open an app!

What are your Energy Zappers? (Please do not answer by naming your spouse, significant other or family members. Addressing those issues is above my pay grade.)

Once you name your Energy Zapper, can you come up with a fix? Strategies from the chapters Maximize Your Return on Time and Maximize Your Return on Spending can be a good starting point.

Ask your friends … you'll be surprised at some of the great fixes you will hear.

A few examples:

> **BRIAN** owned a bunch of season tickets for sporting events and spent a lot of time on Stub Hub getting rid of tickets he wasn't using. What started out as a convenient service became a chore. Sometimes when he was busy, he forgot to sell the tickets. He hated that feeling of wasting time and money! Energy zapped.

> *The solution: Brian decided to get rid of two of his season tickets and just buy tickets for the games he wanted to attend. (He swears it has nothing to do with the Chicago Bears' quarterback situation.)*

> **ANGIE** loved to cook, but always felt a little stressed around 4 pm each day as she started thinking about dinner. She hated running to the grocery store on her way home from work. Not only because it cost her extra time, but also due to the stress of remembering what ingredients she had at home vs. what she needed to buy. Energy zapped.

> *The solution: A food delivery service that fits her family's dietary needs. All the ingredients ready for her to cook! She's been doing this for a few months and her family enjoys the meals. While the service isn't cheap, Angie figures she's actually saving money, as they don't order in or go out as often. And the best part? Her kids enjoy making the dinners with her. As she says, "I paid for fennel and got family time!"*

Can you Zap Your Energy Zapper?

I hope these examples will inspire you to really think about your Energy Zappers. If spending some money will help bring back your energy, you may need to adjust your spending in other areas.

QUESTIONS

Identify your Energy Zappers

Brainstorming with friends is a fun way to find ideas on how to Zap your Energy Zappers.

How you will Zap Your Energy Zapper?

TIME EFFICIENCY TIP FROM ABE LINCOLN

As you become more intentional with your time, you may want to take it a step further. We all have obligations. How can you fulfill these obligations more efficiently? A little advice from Abraham Lincoln can help:

"If I had six hours to chop down a tree,
I would spend the first four hours sharpening the axe."

How true, Honest Abe! It's much more efficient to plan first rather than just jumping in and starting a project.

Too often, instead of taking time to think things through, we rush from one task to the next. Before we know it, we are exhausted and did not accomplish all we set out to do.

Don't underestimate the power of small chunks of time. Even spending 15 minutes making a list, planning your day, or getting organized can save you time. Some of these time-saving tips can also save you some money, a win-win!

Next time you have a big project to complete, remember Abe Lincoln and take some extra time sharpen whatever axe you need to be productive.

THE GIFT OF AIRPLANE MODE

I have a wonderful gift idea … one you can give yourself and that will benefit others. This gift is priceless and won't break your budget!

Give yourself the gift of airplane mode.

I am not talking about your in-flight cell phone setting. I mean putting the phone away, and your computer too. Taking some much-needed time for yourself, being present in the moment, spending uninterrupted time with your friends and family.

Have you ever been completely disconnected? I have and here is my story.

Just a few days of airplane mode did wonders for me.

It started when our daughter decided to spend a semester of her junior year studying in New Zealand. We thought it would be wonderful to visit her, and shockingly she agreed! As we would have to travel halfway around the world, we booked three weeks for the trip. I was excited, but became a bit nervous. Three weeks away … yikes, that's a long time.

I have been working full-time since college and have never taken three weeks off. Don't get me wrong, I'm a big fan of vacations, but most have been a week or so. And trust me, maternity leaves don't count!

I decided to give it a shot and started planning.

I would tie up all the loose ends at work and my non-profit boards before I left. I had full support from my colleagues and clients. New Zealand is 19 hours ahead of Chicago. At 10 am back home it would be 4 am "the next day." I could check in early in the morning if needed. I liked the thought of being a day ahead! Sounded very productive. With Internet access at our hotels, and our international calling plan, I was set. Until …

Stephen suggested we go on a three-day wilderness hike. He showed me three options, all about thirty miles, and told me to choose (guess which one I picked):

HIKE 1:
Carry your own tent, clothes, and food

HIKE 2:
Carry clothes and the company carries
tents and food

HIKE 3:
Carry clothes, and sleep in lodges with
prepared food, running water, and electricity
(Bingo)

Great news. We would be "glamping." I could handle that … I would still have access to my beloved phone and internet.

But then I read the fine print: *Feel free to use your phone for pictures and you can charge the phones at the lodge: Please note that the areas we will be hiking will not have internet or cell access and neither will the lodge. We will have radios for emergencies and you can provide your loved ones with the emergency number.*

After the initial shock, I decided I could go off the grid. Hey, I survived the girls in middle school, what is three days without email and Instagram?

We were given a list of essentials: rain gear, hiking poles, sunscreen, and insect repellent. We trained for the hike by carrying our backpacks around town. We were ready to go.

The Hike Begins

So let's fast forward. We were in New Zealand on our wilderness adventure. The phone went into airplane mode and so did I. We hiked, we laughed, we ate, we played games, my husband and daughter had my undivided attention (when I could catch up to them). I felt so relaxed. Stephen mentioned that it was the first time in years he did not hear me say, "Hang on, just one more email."

What a memorable experience! Sixteen hikers and we were the only Americans. We all bonded as a group. Such interesting people; real characters. Deep, uninterrupted conversations. Nothing to distract us from the beauty of our surroundings.

As we boarded the bus back to Queenstown, I savored the last few hours in airplane mode. And then the announcement came. "You can now have phone access." One of the boys immediately looked up his college grades. Another man dove into his emails. I could see both of their expressions change immediately. We are all so tied to our phones!

It was 2 am in Chicago, so no point in checking right away. I decided to wait. We reached the hotel. I took a long shower and relaxed a bit. Okay, it was time. My heart started to beat a bit faster. I turned off airplane mode and ... over 400 emails!

I scanned them one at a time, and came to the following conclusions:

- Few of them were urgent.

- Those that were urgent had already been resolved by my colleagues.

- I missed a ton of great Black Friday and Cyber Monday deals—great for the budget!

The trip was wonderful in so many ways. We climbed the Sydney Bridge, snorkeled in the Great Barrier Reef, hiked in the Blue Mountains, biked through Sydney, and rafted in Queenstown. Most importantly, we had quality time with our daughter and her friends, as well as our new hiking friends. It was the trip of a lifetime, but the true benefit I received was the wisdom that it's okay to disconnect.

I told a friend about my trip and being disconnected. She said: "I wish my dad would have heard this story. All he did was work, even on vacation. Maybe my parents would still be married today if he was able to break away from work every now and then."

I know life gets busy and we are all tied to our phones. I hope that you will take some time to go in airplane mode. Start with even a few hours and gradually increase your time disconnected. Most phones show you how much time you are spending on them each week. Set a goal for yourself and have your phone alert you when your time is up! You may be surprised what you will learn from this experience.

QUESTIONS

Do you feel present with your loved ones?

Try to go on airplane mode. What was your experience?

TAKEAWAYS

Allocating your time is important, as there is a finite amount available.

Every few months, take a deep look at how you spend your time.

Evaluate what you value most and eliminate spending time on what you don't value.

Clutter can cause stress and cost time and money.

Physical and digital clutter affects our lives.

You won't regret decluttering.

We all have things that zap our energy.

Identify your Energy Zapper and find a solution to zap it.

Brainstorming with friends can help identify ways to zap the Zappers.

There are many benefits to going on airplane mode and being present.

You might be surprised that when you disconnect from technology for a bit, your world won't fall apart. Many tasks can be taken care of by others. Many tasks do not need immediate attention. There are emails you receive that don't need attention at all.

MAXIMIZE
Your Return on Investing and Financial Planning

GOOD FRIENDS, GOOD INVESTORS

An important component to Maximizing Your Return on Life is maximizing your return on investing.

How can you learn what's important when it comes to investing? Take a course? Look for a trusted financial advisor? Both smart ideas (the second one is best). But here's something else to think about. It came to me during a night out with friends.

It was a special evening—just because we were getting together. Delicious food—that night it was Italian—a couple bottles of wine, and of course, such good friends.

I knew them so well. They were also good investors.

Hmm … Good Friends. Good Investors.

**My girlfriends and I all thinking the same thing:
One bottle of wine for 5 of us?**

There had to be a link. Could the same dynamics that help women form such strong friendship bonds help explain the principles that lead to investment success? As we chatted over salad, I thought more about it.

How were we all able to maintain our friendships, keep in touch, support each other, and get together for fun? Particularly when we are juggling families, careers, community service, health and fitness, outside interests? So many people relied on us, yet we figured out a way to be there for each other. It's not always easy, but with a little bit of planning …

Aha! Planning! We're planning experts.

Planning is how we stay in touch. We get those dates set for birthday dinners. We make sure there's time for lunch with friends. We schedule doctor appointments for ourselves and our family. We're the ones who plan the family trips. We are organized and manage the calendar so that everything runs smoothly.

And guess what is the most important concept in reaching your financial goals? It's organization and planning.

These same skills allow us to serve as our family's CFO (Chief Financial Officer). We make sure there is a financial plan in place that deals with saving and investing. We coordinate tax planning with our CPAs, ensure our estate plans are up to date, and deal with insurance and many other key financial items.

Planning allows us to make long-term decisions, such as determining when we can retire and how much we can spend during retirement.

I had to jot it down on the paper tablecloth. I think the crayons that were provided might have been to keep kids occupied, but whatever …

Good friends maintain their bonds through planning.
Good investors reach their goals through planning.

I was beaming as I looked across the table at my friends—some from college, some from childhood. We all have such diverse life experiences to share.

In addition to the friends at the dinner table, I am fortunate to have friends from work, some through my children, and some by way of my husband. Friends from my synagogue and the community. I could go on and on.

As women, we benefit from having a wide variety of friends. We're stronger as a result of the having friends with a diverse set of backgrounds, experiences, and perspectives.

If we have a problem or an issue, chances are somebody in our circle has dealt with it before and can help.

If one of us is down, there is always someone else to pick us up.

Kind of like how bonds "pick up" an investment portfolio when stocks are down. Owning both means you are diversified.

I grabbed my crayon and continued writing. The waiter, looking over my shoulder, tried to figure out what I was doing.

Good friends benefit from diverse life experiences.
Good investors benefit from diversified portfolios.

When I looked up, one of my friends pointed out that a button on my blouse was open. Wow, good friends tell it like it is—no B.S. And you know what? They don't like to listen to B.S. either.

Wait, that's another reason they are good investors! They tune out Wall Street's B.S. The so-called market experts who say they can pick winning stocks. And of course, the predictions of where the markets are headed— where to put your money "now." More B.S. No one has a crystal ball.

My friends know that effective investing starts with broadly diversified funds and long-term thinking, not short-term timing.

I quickly added a third point to my tablecloth diary.

Good friends don't B.S. you.
And they don't listen to Wall Street B.S.

By now it was time to say goodbye (guess who always has the job of allocating the bill?). We had agreed on the restaurant because it had great food and wasn't too expensive. One of my friends had a Groupon as well! We are always talking about where to find a bargain when it comes to food, clothes, what have you. We don't buy anything until we know all of the costs. Wait, you guessed it! That applies to investing too!

Many investors don't know what they are paying for investment advice. There are mutual fund fees, advisory fees, trading costs—all of which can really impact returns. It's important to understand these fees. It's one of the things you *can* control as an investor. Research shows that over time, mutual funds that have lower costs outperform their high-cost counterparts.

That led to my final scribble on the increasingly crowded tablecloth:

> *Good friends love to share a good value.*
> *Good investors keep their costs and taxes low as well.*

I ripped off the section of the tablecloth, stuffed it in my pocket, and hugged my friends.

So much we can learn from each other …

QUESTIONS

How do you feel about your investment strategy?

- Do you have an investment plan?
- Do you understand your investment strategy?
- Do you know the fees you have been paying on your investments?
- Do you have a diversified portfolio?

By the way, have you gotten together with friends lately?

INVESTING CAN MIRROR YOUR FIRST CRUSH

As I got in my Uber to go home, I looked at the torn paper tablecloth with my scribbles. Wow, these were great investing principles to share with my friends.

However, I started thinking about one item left off the napkin. Dealing with the circle of emotions that come with investing. The ups and downs. It reminded me that investing can be as emotional as a first crush.

Do you remember your first crush?

I remember mine. His name was Marc. He was cute, funny, and geographically desirable, since he lived only a block away from me. I remember talking to my friend Myndee about Marc and being really excited.

So how can investing can be emotional as my first crush?

Well, the cycle of investing has five key phases: Optimism, Elation, Nervousness, Fear, and Relief/Stability. Sound familiar? The feelings of a first crush? Let's take a closer look:

1. Optimism

CRUSH
Ah, your first crush. You start to visualize the two of you together. That's when you go ahead and tell your best friend. You wonder if your crush likes you too. This is when I had Detective Myndee do some investigating.

INVESTING

You budget well and now have some extra cash to invest. It's been a good market, so you call your financial advisor to add funds to your portfolio. You are optimistic that this will be a great decision.

2. Elation

CRUSH

You've finally heard the news from your friend: Your crush likes you back! What a magical moment full of elation. Everything feels wonderful and you couldn't be happier. Maybe after school you guys can hang out! Life is beautiful.

INVESTING

You have been watching the news and the market continues to go up. You meet with your financial advisor and it has been a great quarter. Your investment portfolio is up. What a feeling! You've made the right decision.

3. Nervousness turns to fear

CRUSH

Just when things seem like they couldn't be better, all of the sudden you hear rumors that your crush might like someone else. Oh no! You get more than a little nervous. You question yourself in countless ways: *"Did I do the right thing? Should I really have told Myndee that I had a crush on Marc? Will I be able to face Marc at school?"*

INVESTING

Things are going smoothly, with the markets heading up, up, up. Unfortunately, one day bad news surfaces and your portfolio takes a dip. Nervousness takes over as you ask yourself, *"Did I do the right thing? Should I have waited and kept the money in cash?"*

Just as Myndee helped calm me down, talking to an advisor during tough markets can also ease your nerves. Someone who can help you remember the big picture through the market's ups and downs, giving great advice like, "Stay the course, markets come back over time."

4. Relief and Stability

CRUSH
Good news! As it turns out, Marc didn't really like the other girl after all. He liked me! What a relief.

INVESTING
The market recovers and you feel good about your original investment: *"Why was I so emotional?"*

Lessons to be learned from both your first crush and investing

- There are going to be ups and downs.

- The experiences can be emotional.

- Having a close friend or a financial advisor by your side is crucial.

Does this bring back memories for you as well? You and I both know that first crushes rarely work out. However, unlike your first crush, working with a trusted financial advisor can result in a long-term relationship.

QUESTIONS

Do you have a strategy to handle your emotions?

EXTRA CREDIT:

Call your first crush to "catch up."
I called mine.
I am even going to give him a copy of my book.

WHERE ARE YOUR FINANCIAL GAS STATIONS?

W hen we go on vacation and the car is running low on gas, my husband always seems to push the vehicle to the limit. If you were listening in our car, you would hear...

SHARI:
Stephen, maybe we should stop for gas over there.
We're at about a quarter of a tank left.

STEPHEN:
Shari, stop worrying. We'll be fine.

Fifteen minutes later …

SHARI:
Stephen, we're out in the countryside. Maybe we should check Waze.
There may not be another gas station close by.

STEPHEN:
Shari, stop worrying. We'll be fine.

Ten minutes later …

STEPHEN:
Umm, Shari, we may have a problem.

SHARI:
Who could have known?*
Comment has been edited to remove profanity.

If only he could plan ahead and know where the gas stations were on our trip, we could eliminate a major source of stress, one that's totally avoidable.

Stephen, "E" does not stand for enough!

Having cash reserves for an emergency is like have a having a full tank of gas.

Cash Reserves = Full Tank = Lower Stress

Creating Your Cash Reserves

So, as always, the best way to get started … is to get started. Create a rainy-day fund.

Sometimes it's **the act of simply putting some money aside on a regular basis, regardless of the amount, that creates a good habit and sense of discipline.** Start with what feels comfortable to you. Saving can be liberating and uplifting in itself. You're doing something!

What if you don't have the luxury of saving a portion of each paycheck? You may have just started working, or you're paying off student loans or have children's expenses and/or college or, well, money's just tight.

You still need to have access to funds in an emergency.

Here are other ways to help you access cash in an emergency:

- Do you have equity in your home? Consider a home equity line of credit. Set it up at a time when you don't need it. Then it will be there when you do. Again, this should be a short-term solution for a cash crunch, not for long-term debt.

- Do you have an investment account at a brokerage firm? You can temporarily borrow against your account. This is called margin debt. Of course, have a plan to pay down this margin debt.

- Do you have cash value in a life insurance policy? You may be able to borrow or withdraw the cash value— always check on the tax consequences.

- Many 401(k) plans allow you to borrow against your balance. Understand the terms—how much you can borrow and what the rate is. And, most importantly, have a plan to pay back a loan as quickly as possible. I'm not advocating borrowing from your retirement savings as a long-term or first option, mind you, but you should know whether it's available.

- Do you have family or friends who you can genuinely rely on for emergencies? Just knowing someone can pitch in can ease your mind.

Please, please, *please* try to avoid using credit cards as your source of emergency spending. It's tempting to think, "Well, I'm sure I can pay them off when I …" But the "when I" never seems to happen. You can quickly find yourself caught in a cycle of high balances and high interest rates.

Having cash reserves gives you a feeling of quiet confidence. It's comforting to know that you have budgeted for non-budget items, especially as you continue to save and invest for the big-picture things—a home, college, retirement, etc.

The time to think about where you will get cash in an emergency is **now**!

QUESTIONS

Do you have a rainy-day fund?

Do you know the rates and terms of borrowing from your 401(k) plan?

Do you have a home equity line? What is the rate?

Know the cash value in your life insurance policies.

Where would you be able to access money in an emergency? Plan now!

EIGHT ITEMS TO START NOW

To maximize your return on investing and financial planning, here are eight must-complete items. Since it is easy to procrastinate, I am giving you an eight-week challenge. You can make it easy on yourself by doing one a week. Or you can make it hard and wait until week eight. Your call.

We have an expression in our office when a client asks, "What's the best way to get started?" We simply say: *START NOW.*

WEEK #1:
Schedule your doctors' appointments.

People are counting on you. Here is a list of nonnegotiable doctors' appointments.

- Annual physical exam

- Dentist

- Gynecologist

- Dermatologist

- Mammogram

- Colonoscopy: not a crowd pleaser but important

- Specialists

Put the book down and make the calls. Schedule the appointments. One idea is to pick a time of year—the month before your birthday, March 15, etc., and schedule the date in your calendar to make all your doctors' appointments for the year. Another alternative is to schedule your next appointment when you leave the current one.

~ Extra Credit (Week #1) ~

When you have made all of your appointments, schedule some special time for yourself, maybe a long walk or a yoga class. Put it in your calendar.

WEEK #2:
Get (or update) a healthcare power of attorney.

It's a straightforward document that designates someone (your "agent") to make decisions about your medical treatment if you are unable to do so. It also covers end-of-life decisions.

And while you are completing your own healthcare powers of attorney, complete the same for your children over 18. Trust me on how important this is. Remember when my daughter tore her ACL and I tried to talk to the doctor? He would not give me—her mom—any information unless I sent the healthcare power of attorney!

~ Extra Credit (Week #2) ~

Once you have healthcare powers of attorney complete, provide a copy to your agent.

WEEK #3:
Get your estate plan done (or updated).

Call your estate planning attorney. If you don't have one, ask another trusted advisor for a recommendation.

Your estate plan provides instructions on how your assets should be distributed upon your death. It also can make arrangements to appoint guardians for minor children. You can also designate charitable donations. If you have an estate plan, when was the last time you updated it? Are you sure it still reflects your wishes?

~ Extra Credit (Week #3) ~
Once your estate plan is completed, take that extra step and make sure that all your investment accounts and real estate holdings are titled correctly and all your retirement accounts have proper beneficiaries.

WEEK #4:
Consider life, disability, and long-term care insurance

Death or disability are devastating to families. Financial stress should not be added at a most difficult time.

Call a trusted insurance professional to determine how much life, disability, and long-term care insurance you need. Get it in place. You'll sleep better at night.

Term insurance is relatively inexpensive. Premiums are usually a set amount annually for a given number of years. An example is a 30-year, $1 million dollar policy. At the end of 30 years, the policy expires or the premiums may increase.

Disability insurance is often overlooked, yet it can be life-changing and is often needed more than life insurance. What if you were to be disabled and could not work? Would your family be covered? Living expenses, mortgage, college ... the list goes on.

Long-term care insurance can be beneficial. It can be quite expensive, so it's important to consider the costs vs. potential benefit.

~ Extra Credit (Week #4) ~
Review your insurance needs,
and the cost of your premiums, every few years,
as your circumstances will change.

Week #5:
Start a Savings Plan

Please don't wait until you get that raise. Don't wait for your kids to finish college. Save what you can, but start saving.

THE TWO MAIN SAVINGS VEHICLES:

RETIREMENT SAVINGS: The annual additions to your retirement accounts, including 401(k) contributions, employer matches, IRA contributions, etc.

INVESTMENT SAVINGS: The annual additions to your non-retirement accounts, such as bank or money market accounts, investment/brokerage accounts, college savings accounts, and other investments. To make it easier, set up a direct transfer each month.

SET AN ANNUAL SAVINGS GOAL:

RETIREMENT SAVINGS   _____

INVESTMENT SAVINGS   _____

TOTAL ANNUAL SAVINGS   _____

~ *Extra Credit (Week #5)* ~

Check that you are putting away at least enough in your 401(k) plan to receive the maximum match from your employer.

An employer match is free money—your employer "matches" your contribution up to a certain amount.
So take advantage of it!

Week #6:
Know Your Assets and Liabilities

These are very important numbers, and you should keep track of them on a regular basis. You should also understand the trends. Let's go through each.

ASSETS

LIQUID: Accounts that can be turned into cash right away: money market accounts, checking/savings accounts

_____

_____

_____

INVESTMENT ASSETS: Brokerage and retirement accounts holding stocks and bonds, as well as other long-term investments such as rental real estate or illiquid partnerships

_____

_____

_____

PERSONAL ASSETS: Your home (use the market value), autos, and other big-ticket items such as jewelry.

_____

_____

_____

LIABILITIES

Liabilities represent debt to be repaid. Don't include credit card balances that are paid in full at the end of each month.

REAL ESTATE DEBT

Home mortgage balance: _____

Home equity line balance: _____

CREDIT CARDS

Balances not paid off monthly: _____

OTHER LOANS

Student loans balance: _____

Business loans balance: _____

Personal loans balance: _____

TOTAL LIABILITIES _____

~ *Extra Credit (Week #6)* ~

Look at all your liabilities. What are the minimum payments? What are the interest rates? Pay off the highest rate loans first, usually credit card debt. Set up a plan to reduce your debt. When it is paid off, take the amount you had been allocating toward repaying debt and redirect it towards savings.

Week #7:
Plan for Your Retirement

I'm not just talking about financial projections on sources of income and spending during retirement. These projections are important, and you should have a full financial plan taking into account your assets and your spending, but there is more to retirement planning than just numbers.

What I mean is ask yourself … *What do I want my retirement to look like? How am I going to spend my time?*

Visualizing what you want your retirement to look like is a fantastic exercise as you plan for these precious years. Retirement is not all or nothing. You may continue to work but at a different job than the past 30 years. Explore your passions. Start planning your retirement while you are still working.

~ *Extra Credit (Week #7)* ~

Understand and evaluate your options when regarding when to begin taking Social Security, as well as Medicare plans.

Week #8:
Organize Important Documents

What would happen if someone needed to step in and take care of your financial affairs or manage your healthcare? Would they have access to the necessary information?

Here is a list of important documents and contact information:

PERSONAL RECORDS

- Contact information for relatives, friends, and business relationships
- Medical records
- Contact information for doctors, pharmacies
- Health insurance/Medicare card
- Birth certificates: yours and your children's
- Passports
- Marriage certificate
- Safe-deposit box key
- Other legal documents: adoption, divorce, military, citizenship, custody

LEGAL, ESTATE PLANNING, AND TAXES

- Contact information for professionals
- Wills/Trusts
- Health Care Power of Attorney
- Property Power of Attorney
- Burial/cremation instructions
- Funeral arrangements
- Instructions to executor

- Death certificates
- Home title
- Other real estate deeds
- Vehicle titles
- Mortgage/home equity line papers
- Inventory/appraisal of art/jewelry/collections
- Prior years' tax returns
- Business tax returns
- Property tax records

BUSINESS

- Contact information for professionals
- Partnership, LLC, S Corp Agreements
- Buy/sell agreements

INSURANCE

- Contact information for professionals
- Health insurance
- Life insurance
- Disability insurance
- Personal liability insurance
- Business insurance

BANKING, SAVINGS, INVESTMENT, RETIREMENT, 529 COLLEGE SAVINGS ACCOUNTS, AND CREDIT CARD ACCOUNTS

- Institution
- Title
- Account number

CHARITABLE

- Pledges

- Donor-Advised Fund information

PASSWORDS:

- Make sure one other person has access to important ones

~ Extra Credit (Week #8) ~

Share the location of these documents with your loved ones.

EIGHT WEEKS. That's two months to get these items completed. You will feel great when you are done. Starting is the hardest part.

Now get going!

QUESTIONS

What items are priorities for you to complete?

Establish a schedule to complete these items.

Celebrate when items are completed!

TEARS AND TARGET DATE FUNDS:
GIVING 401(K) ADVICE TO OUR DAUGHTER

Our daughter Isabel started her first job at Deloitte as an auditor. Okay, before she corrects me, an Audit and Assurance Associate! Stephen and I could not be prouder.

Now that she has a paycheck coming in, we encouraged her to create a budget and live within her means. I reminded her of what my dad, Dante Greco, always told me: "You can have anything you want, but you can't have everything you want."

During her first week of work she was inundated with employee benefit choices. Now, Isabel is very independent, usually making all of her decisions on her own. However, she decided that Stephen and I perhaps could add some value when it came to her 401(k)!

Our first piece of advice was to contribute as much as she could to take advantage of the company's match. Her company, like many others, will match a percentage of her contributions, up to a certain portion of her salary. That's free money—so she needed to take advantage of that.

Now it was time to choose among the investment choices. We guided her to the Vanguard Target Retirement Fund option.

Target funds are all-in-one diversified funds designed to manage risk over time. When retirement is far-off, the funds have high exposure to stocks, and over time, as the retirement date gets closer, the allocation shifts to less in stocks and more in bonds. These funds also have rock-bottom costs as the underlying investments are index funds, which we love!

We advised her to select Vanguard 2060 Target Date Fund. Isabel asked, "What does the 2060 target date mean?" Stephen explained that 2060 would be about when she would look to retire.

"2060!" she exclaimed! "That's 40 years from now … OMG, that's a long time to work!"

My baby girl was right. I started to get emotional, teary-eyed. The next stage of her life was beginning. All I could say was welcome to the real world, Isabel. It's not so bad.

And the real world is lucky to have you, as are we. Don't worry about the 40 years. As they say, the days are long but the years go by quickly. And if you love what you do, like me, the job doesn't feel like work.

You go girl.

IS YOUR DEBT UNHAPPY?

Does your credit card frown at you when it comes out of your wallet? Has your mortgage statement ever broken out in tears? You're not alone. Fortunately, Dr. Shari Reiches has completed the following research study on this small but growing phenomena in the world of financial planning: UDD (Unhappy Debt Disorder).

UNHAPPY DEBT DISORDER: CONSEQUENCES OF LACK OF ATTENTION

Research Participants:

Mr. Christopher Credit Card
Ms. Mollie Mortgage

Research Goal:

Analyze the impact of attention given
two common forms of household debt.

Methodology:

Dr. Reiches reviewed the time, attention, and follow-up
given to these examples of credit card and mortgage debt,
including review of interest rates and plans to lower balances.

Results/Findings:

- Mr. Christopher Credit Card was diagnosed with UDD—Unhappy Debt Disorder, due to lack of attention.

Symptoms:

- He is often ignored by his owner.

- His owner has no control over Mr. Credit Card's interest rate, and doesn't even realize it is in the high teens. Mr. Credit Card's response, "It's like my owner forgot my birthday. Sad."

- Mr. Credit Card's balance has gained weight over the last several months, with no plan in place to slim down.

Proposed Treatment Plan:

- Mr. Credit Card should have a "heart-to-card" discussion with his owner.

- Owner should make a list of all credit card debt and come up with a plan to pay it down over a certain time period, starting with the highest interest rate cards.

- Mr. Credit Card should encourage his owner to go on a low-shopping diet to reduce spending while paying down debt.

Results/Findings:

- Ms. Mollie Mortgage was given a clean bill of health:
- Her owner pays lots of attention to her—she was recently refinanced at an extremely low rate.

- Ms. Mollie Mortgage is slowly slimming down, with her owner using extra cash as it becomes available to pay down principal.

Summary

Debt that is not given proper attention is subject to UDD—Unhappy Debt Disorder. Help reduce the symptoms of UDD by paying off your credit card balance each month. If you do maintain a balance, know the interest rate and come up with a plan to pay it off. Next, take a look at your mortgage. Now is an excellent time to review its terms and possibly refinance at a lower rate.

About the Participants and Author

The names of the participants have been changed to protect their anonymity. You should diagnosis your own debt's happiness, and your results may vary from test subjects.

Shari Greco Reiches is not an MD, but she cares a lot about your financial health.

TAKEAWAYS

Your friendships can teach you about the core principles of investing.

Having a good financial plan, diversifying your portfolio, avoiding the media hype, and keeping fees and taxes low can lead to a successful investment experience.

It's important to handle your emotions as an investor. Emotions often get in the way of a good financial plan.

Having a cash reserve can reduce stress.

The following can provide needed funds in an emergency:

- Rainy-day fund
- Your brokerage account
- Home Equity Line of credit
- Borrowing from your 401(k) account
- Friends/family

TAKEAWAYS, *continued*

Start Now. The eight must-complete items:

- Schedule your doctors' appointments
- Get (or update) your healthcare power of attorney
- Get your estate planning done (or updated)
- Consider life, disability, and long-term care insurance
- Start a savings plan
- Know your assets and liabilities
- Plan for your retirement
- Organize important documents

It's important to start investing early. A 401(k) account is a great start.

Pay attention to your debt. Know the interest rates and terms.

MAXIMIZE
the Return on Life
for Your Loved Ones

TEACH YOUR CHILDREN WELL

An oldie but goodie. Though I doubt Crosby, Stills, Nash & Young were thinking of finances when they wrote this song, we want to teach our children well when it comes to money.

With my dad being a banker, money talk was part of our dinner conversation. He taught me how to read the stock market pages in the newspaper when I was 13 years old. I understand this is not the case in most families.

It is never too early to teach your children good financial habits. Here are some of the things we taught our kids, starting at an early age:

1) SPEND THOUGHTFULLY

When our kids were little and we went on vacation, we gave each daughter an allowance for the entire trip. They could use the money for souvenirs, food, clothes, or anything else they wanted. It was their money to spend, no questions asked. We made it clear: that's it and there is no more! The first time we did this, one daughter spent all her money at the airport and unsuccessfully pleaded for more. Our other daughter came home with all her money. Two extremes! Over time, they both learned real-world lessons on how to budget.

2) THE VALUE OF HARD WORK

We started our daughters off with the concept of working for an allowance. Old fashioned chores such as folding laundry. Next we encouraged them to do chores for the neighbors (shoveling, dog watching, etc.). When they reached age 16, we pushed them to get jobs. All of these things provided them with a real sense of pride and ownership. Even today, with kids being overscheduled with school activities and homework, encourage them to find time for a paying job. And then guess what? With that ownership, usually they'll want to protect and save their money a bit more. Which brings me to the third strategy…

3) THE VALUE OF SAVING

We opened savings accounts for our children to deposit their hard-earned money. We had them make regular deposits, perhaps a portion of their allowance. They liked to watch their money grow. They began to appreciate the power of savings and compound interest, as well as how to put aside money for a rainy day or work towards a special purchase. Better yet, they learned to rely on this account as their source of funds for spending (instead of coming to us all the time). They started to understand the concept that they couldn't spend what they didn't have. We empowered them to face the consequences of their spending and savings decisions.

Now, these aren't the *only* things we've taught our daughters in regard to money:

- We said "no" to them when they asked for things we thought were extravagant.

- We taught them about borrowing, credit cards, and the risks involved in carrying a balance. Most importantly, we taught them the importance of living within your means.

- We've been transparent about major purchases so they could see how we saved and researched the best prices.

There is so much to teach our children as they grow into young adults. However, starting with the above three strategies, you'll be providing them a solid financial foundation.

- Spend some time talking about money with your children.

- Help your young adults with budgeting and investment decisions.

- Encourage your young adults to save.

GIVE YOUR CHILDREN SKIN IN THE GAME

When my children were young, I was building my wealth management career. I was very fortunate to have wonderful support network: my husband, parents, other family members, a caregiver (same one for over 12 years!), and of course, my friends.

There were times I had client meetings at night and worked late. I explained to my daughters that some clients could only meet after work and I was building my business. Bringing in new clients often required these meetings. They understood.

How could I have my daughters invested in my success? We had a family meeting and I explained that they might need to do some extra chores when I was not home. The good news—my salary increased each time I brought in a new client, which benefitted the whole family.

I asked them what they would consider a good reward for their help. They both agreed to Dave & Buster's gift cards. Since we were in this together and they had an impact on my success, they would earn a $5 dollar Dave & Buster's gift card with every new client.

We made a chart to keep track of new clients (no names, of course). A tick mark for each one. We all high-fived with every success. If I called home to check in and told them I was working late, Isabel would say, "That's okay, Mom, as long as you are working on a new client."

One year I was having a tough quarter with new business. There were no recent tick marks on the chart. As I was eating breakfast one morning my daughter looked at me, then the chart, and said, "Mom, umm not so much happening with new clients lately. What's up with that?"

Wow! Not only was I receiving pressure from my boss, but from my daughter as well! I had to laugh. I explained to her that it takes time for hard work to pay off. I hoped to quickly add a tick mark to the chart.

As I added the next several new clients, we enjoyed a trip to Dave & Buster's as a family. Their next financial lesson was how to allocate their winning tickets for prizes, but you will have to wait for my next book for that story.

Teaching my daughters their first business lesson.

We often discussed that this was a team effort and that everyone had a part in helping me grow my business. Even today, they ask me how things are going and congratulate me as the business grows. Of course, we talk about their jobs as well.

QUESTION

Is there a way to include your children in your passions?

A LETTER TO LEAH:
ADVICE FOR A RECENT COLLEGE GRAD

When grads begin their first job, the habits they start as young adults will have an impact for years to come. The following is a letter I wrote to my partner David Rappaport's daughter Leah, upon her college graduation, sharing some life lessons.

Leah is a special young woman. At 18 months old she was diagnosed as being on the autism spectrum. She worked hard to meet her challenges, and graduated Magna Cum Laude with a degree in Mathematics from Carthage College. Upon graduation, she started work at Aspiritech, a non-profit company that hires adults on the autism spectrum to provide software testing and quality assurance services to corporate clients across the U.S.

Dear Leah,

Congratulations on your graduation and new job. We are all so proud of you. You had many challenges to overcome and you did it with hard work, determination, and a cheerful attitude. What an accomplishment!

I have known you for the past 20 years and it has been a joy to see you grow up. You are now entering the next, exciting phase of your life, and I'd like to offer a few thoughts (some financial, some not so much) about starting out on the right track. After all, I'm in the advice business.

So, enjoy my Top Ten List for recent college grads. (There are actually 11 items because I am all about giving more than what's expected—and think you are too.)

SHARI'S TOP TEN LIST FOR COLLEGE GRADS

1. Get started with that first job—don't be too picky.

Dr. Seuss said:
"You're off to Great Places!
Today is your day!
Your mountain is waiting,
So... get on your way!"

NOT
"Hang out 'til your dream job
Lands in your lap.
And 'til that day comes...
Nothing wrong with a nap."

Your first job teaches you responsibility, the value of hard work, and the necessity of teamwork. So take that job and get started. You can move up from there.

2. Always come to work with a good attitude

No problem for you, Leah, always with your sunny outlook! Remember, your job is to make your boss's job easier. Be on time, dress the part, have a smile on your face, shake hands firmly, turn off your phone, and work hard.

Develop a reputation early for getting things done, and that reputation will stick with you for a long time. If you do these things, the other job requirements will fall into place.

As my first supervisor at Arthur Andersen said, "You should be at work five minutes before your boss and leave five minutes after your boss."

Please don't ask me, "Arthur who?"

3. Understand your total compensation package

Salary is one component of your total "comp." You should understand other benefits, such as health insurance, 401(k) retirement saving plans, and bonuses. Companies often offer creative benefits such as stock options, life and disability insurance, and even discounts on health club memberships.

Take the time to understand your full package and ask questions if you need help. It all may be a little confusing at first, but those benefits are for you. Take advantage of them.

4. Know what comes out of your paycheck before you see a dime

Guess what—your salary divided by 26 pay periods in a year does not equal your paycheck. There is money withheld for all sorts of stuff: retirement account contributions (more on that to come!), taxes, health insurance, etc.

Make sure that you have the proper amount withheld for income taxes. Again, ask for help if you need it.

And another congratulations is due—you are now paying into our Social Security and Medicare system. Really, your dad thanks you, because he's not that far off from ... Anyway, understand each box on your paycheck stub— including the taxes you are paying.

5. Pay yourself first

Saving for retirement forty-plus years away may seem like an odd concept, but you have such an advantage—time. Get started now. Contribute as much as you can to your 401(k)—your employer may match your contributions up to a certain percentage. That's free money, so strive to get the full matching amount. Other savings options include Roth IRAs, and non-retirement investment accounts as well.

Start building that rainy-day start investing early, stay disciplined, think long-term, and you'll do great.

P.S. Your dad will help with the investment selections for your 401(k) plan. Take his advice—he's pretty smart.

6. Have a plan for spending

I know you will live at home initially. Smart. Here are some other smart thoughts to get you started.

Have a plan for your paycheck that puts you in control. I've seen too many young adults spend without a plan in place, and that leads to problems—credit card debt or constantly asking a parent for help.

Start with a realistic budget. You are good at math, so this should be fun for you. Remember: You can have anything you want, but not everything you want, so spend carefully.

7. Keep a clean credit record and check your credit annually

It is important that you start establishing credit. Open a credit card account—one with low fees. Never keep a balance. Always pay off your credit card each month. That means on time. Are you forgetful? Then set up an automatic payment system for your bills—but check each purchase to make sure it's legit.

Don't forget to check your credit annually through a free service such as annualcreditreport.com.

8. Clean up and check your social media

We are Facebook friends and I love all your posts and pictures. Continue to keep it clean! Don't be surprised that potential employers will be taking a look. Your LinkedIn account also looks great. Love your picture. You go girl! Try to increase your connections on LinkedIn and review it often to keep informed about your friends and future contacts. I just sent you an invitation to connect. Please accept it promptly.

It's never too early to think about networking. Keep in touch with your friends and contacts from school and elsewhere. Be helpful to them as they begin their journeys as well.

9. Don't forget about your Health Care Power of Attorney

I know you filled out this form when you turned 18. Good job! It lets health care providers know who can make decisions for you in case of an emergency, etc. Remind your parents or whoever you have chosen to keep this in a safe place.

I realize it's not the first thing that comes up when you are hanging out with your friends, but encourage them to have one as well.

10. Invest in your values and yourself

This may be the most important to-do of all. Too many young people (well, maybe older folks as well) focus their time, energy, and money on keeping up with the lifestyles of those who surround them. They see friends with new cars, clothes, jewelry, vacations, etc. In the long run, all that stuff isn't what brings happiness or contentment.

Investing in yourself means continually expanding your skills and staying up to date on trends in your profession. Education does not stop with a college degree.

Spend some time thinking about what is important to you. Maybe it's spending quality time with those you love, or giving back to your community. I understand how much it meant to you to volunteer your time and raise funds for cancer research. Keep up your wonderful efforts. It is part of who you are.

In addition to helping others, do take care of yourself. A health club membership isn't an extravagance if you use it—it's an investment in your continued wellness. And the occasional mani & pedi, well, that's okay too!

11. Call your parents and grandparents

I know this is a time of independence and finding your way, but your parents and relatives will play an important part in this journey. They enjoy your calls and texts more than you can imagine. I know you're busy, but even a quick hello will make their day!

They are so proud of you and truly look forward to the time they spend with you. Time flies, so cherish the time you have with your parents. You are lucky—they are pretty great people.

Leah, I can't put into words how proud of you I am today. I enjoy when you call looking for your dad. When we talk, you always take the time to ask about Maddie and Isabel. I also love seeing that big smile on your face.

Keep that smile, because over the years ahead you'll face your share of tough days. But don't forget there will be more good ones than bad ones. And you have friends and family to see you through the rough times. Always.

Leah, so proud of you!

I know you will be a success at anything you put your mind to. I can't wait to see the next chapter of your life!

Love,
Shari

P.S. When you see Maddie and Isabel remind them about #11.

PASSING YOUR VALUES
(IN ADDITION TO THE TURKEY)

We can't take for granted the time we spend together as a family. Holidays are a good time to share your values and what is important to you.

We tried something a little different one Thanksgiving—one of my favorite holidays.

That year, Isabel came home from school in Denver and Maddie came home from Kansas City. I get so excited to have all of us under one roof.

The beds were made, the refrigerator was stocked, and a bunch of old clothes were in boxes waiting for us to decide what to keep and what to donate. (Why not use a long weekend as an opportunity to declutter?)

That Thanksgiving was even more special than most, as I hosted for the first time in 20 years. Twenty-four people at my home! I had to fight with other relatives for this, and I won! Never mind that I lost the last 19 years. My mom came early and helped me and my girls prepare the meal. Three generations cooking together. I'm getting emotional thinking about it. And hungry.

In addition to catching up and eating, I wanted my family to use this gathering as an opportunity to discuss their values.

I sent the following note to everyone so they could think about what they want to discuss.

- Tell a family story, especially about someone who is not with us anymore.

- What was a big decision point in your life? How did your values guide your decision?

- Who made a difference in your life when you needed a helping hand?

- What tradition or values do you most want to continue in your family?

I was surprised by some of the answers we shared. We all learned a lot. And, oh did we laugh at some of the stories.

I encourage you to do the same with your family. It could be at holiday dinner or a weekend when everyone is together.

It may take a while for the conversation to get started, but based on my experience, it will be rewarding for everyone. One more thing—get that phone out and press that red *record video* button. It will be a treasure for future generations.

Mom and Sam are all smiles. The turkey was perfect!

Your Values in Action

Your family will enjoy discussing values at Thanksgiving, or at any meal or gathering. That's a great start. But don't forget, actions speak louder than words. Your children are observing and learning from you every day. Are you kind to strangers? Do you speak out against injustice? Help other family members?

How do you support your community? What charities do you give time and money to? Your children will see the gifts you are giving others—your time and money based on your values. I'll bet they will do the same.

In the Jewish religion we call this *L'Dor V'dor*—passing down from one generation to the next.

When the next generation models your values, it's an incredible feeling.

TAKEAWAYS

It is never too early to teach your children about money.

Make learning about money fun and use strategies they can understand.

Good money habits continue as your children become young adults.

Take time to share your Core Values with your family and loved ones.

Sharing your Core Values will impact future generations.

MAXIMIZE
Your Return with Gratitude

LESSONS FROM A FISHERMAN

W hen I first started my Rappaport Reiches Capital Management, my brother Adam asked me about my goals. "Grow, grow, grow, I want the business to grow!" I said. "Well, why is growth so important?" he asked. I thought, isn't it obvious? But then, he shared a parable that got me thinking:

> A banker was taking a much-needed vacation in a small coastal village. One afternoon, while walking on the beach, he came across a fisherman docking his small boat, full of the day's haul. The banker was impressed by the quality of the fish and asked how long it took to catch them. The fisherman replied, "A few hours." The banker then asked why he didn't stay out longer and catch more fish. The fisherman replied that he had enough to support his family's needs. The banker inquired, "What do you do with the rest of your time?" The fisherman replied, "I take a nap, play with my children, read, and watch the sunset while sipping wine with my wife."
>
> The banker scoffed. "I have an Ivy League MBA, and I can help you. You should spend more time fishing and with the extra proceeds buy a bigger boat. Over time, with the increased catch from the bigger boat you could buy several boats and hire fishermen to work for you. Eventually you would have a whole fleet of fishing boats. Instead of selling your catch to the people in your

village, you could own your own cannery and grow an enterprise."

The fisherman asked, "How long will this all take?"

To which the banker replied, "Fifteen to twenty years. It will take some sacrifice—late nights, borrowed money, risk along the way."

"But what then?" asked the fisherman.

The banker laughed and said, "That's the best part. When the time is right you would sell your company and become very rich. You would make millions."

"Millions? Then what?"

"Why then you could retire. You could fish for a few hours, take a nap, play with your children and grand-children, read, and watch the sunset while sipping wine with your wife," replied the banker.

"But aren't I doing that now?"

A smart fisherman indeed.

As for me, well, I'm grateful that my firm has grown, but over time I've come to realize that growth was not really my number one goal for our business. It was helping others.

I love to see stress leave clients' faces as we organize their financial lives. I get emotional as I share in their satisfaction and relief when they realize the plan we set in place years ago works—they can retire and live the life they want to live.

I enjoy helping people maximize their return on life. That helps me maximize mine.

Out walking with my brother Adam.
I always value his advice.

PRACTICE GRATITUDE

As you continue your journey to maximize your return on life, it's important to take time along the way to reflect on the things you are thankful for. To practice gratitude as part of your daily routine.

Too often we are engulfed by current events. How can we not be? We feel the weight of the world on our shoulders. We forget about the good that surrounds us. The people that love us.

Savor, absorb and really pay attention to the good things in your life. A family birthday celebration, a good meal, a stunning sunrise, time laughing with friends.

Take some time to hone in on these things. Maybe even right now. I'm a list person, so my first thought is to make a list of five things to be grateful for and keep this list handy during difficult times. Talk about it. Share it. Update it. And most importantly, act on it.

What are your five?

1. _____

2. _____

3. _____

4. _____

5. _____

Rekindle a Relationship

Rekindling a lapsed relationship is one of the most powerful, heart-warming things you can do to practice gratitude. Chances are the other person has been thinking about you as well.

Here are some ways to do that:

- Call an old friend. Don't worry about the time that's already passed since your last conversation. You can make up for that in an instant by reaching out. You don't need a reason other than to say, "I just wanted to know how you're doing."

- Call your parents. Let them know how grateful you are for their love and support. If they are not around, call someone else's parents. Someone is out there whose face will brighten!

- Tell each of your family members, or whoever is in your immediate orbit, something special about themselves. Don't worry about being eloquent. The sillier the better. Capturing small (even quirky) details about a loved one is one of the best ways to show you care. And have a laugh together.

- Call that distant relative. They may be shocked! You may be shocked! Catch up. It's been awhile. Following them on Facebook doesn't count.

- Check in on a neighbor. If they are elderly or have trouble getting around, offer to buy groceries or anything else they need.

- Track down one of your former teachers. Say hello and give them an update on your life. Let them know how much you appreciated what they did for you. Mention how much you enjoyed their class.

- Reach out to someone special. Someone who impacted your life. I'll leave the details up to you.

QUESTIONS

Who did you show your gratitude to?

How did it feel?

TAKEAWAYS

We can learn a lot from the fisherman.

Take the time to practice gratitude.

Reconnect with someone special in your life.

How Will You
MAXIMIZE
Your Return on Life?

SAM'S STORY:
CHECK IN ON YOURSELF

S am was at a coffee shop and politely asked Ms. Miller at the next table if she minded if he made a quick call. She told him sure, go ahead. Sam called Mr. Jones.

SAM:
Mr. Jones, I live in the neighborhood and was wondering if you would like someone to shovel your driveway this winter.

MR. JONES:
I already have someone taking care of that for me.

SAM:
Are you happy with the service provided?

MR. JONES:
I am very happy. He did a great job last year,
but thank you for asking.

SAM:
Thank you for your time. Perhaps I'll check in next year.

Sam went back to working on his computer. Ms. Miller then started chatting with him.

MS. MILLER:

I understand you might be looking for some shoveling work this winter. I could use someone and would be happy to hire you.

SAM:

Thank you for your interest, but I am booked solid.

MS. MILLER:

If you are so busy, why did you call Mr. Jones looking for work?

SAM:

Oh, you see, I am the one who does the shoveling for Mr. Jones and I wanted to check in to make sure I was doing a good job.

I heard a version of this story at our High Holiday services this year. The Jewish New Year is a time for reflection.

Every now and then we need to take the time to check in on ourselves. Be honest! Schedule the time. And make sure along the way that you …

- **Embrace your successes.** What went well? What did you do that provided a sense of accomplishment? Were you able to reduce some stress? Add more time?

- **Understand your challenges.** What were some difficulties along the way? What did you put off doing? Did you set a goal and have trouble achieving it?

- **Make a plan.** Don't be too hard on yourself. Today is a new day to get it done.

- **Set a time of year to check in on yourself.**

MARY'S STORY:
USING HER CORE VALUES TO GUIDE LIFE'S DECISIONS

H ere's an example of how my client, Mary, has used several of the principles we have discussed to Maximize Her Return on Life.

Mary is smart and successful. She has an MBA and was a senior HR executive at a large corporation. As the sole provider for her financial security, Mary worked full time for over 30 years. She has been disciplined and saved quite a bit.

Last year, her company was sold and her job was eliminated. She thought she would quickly update her resume and start the new job search. She was on auto-pilot and knew what steps to take, such as *get started yesterday!* I felt it might benefit Mary to slow down. We talked quite a bit and I encouraged her to think about her Core Values.

Here is her list, including how she defines each item:

Love:
Connecting to others in a positive, loving way.

Respect:
Embracing people for who they are
and treating them like you'd like to be treated.

Authenticity:
Working from the heart and staying true to yourself.

Growth:
Always striving to learn more and get to the next level.

Community:
Sharing your wisdom and experiences; learning from others.

With her list in hand, auto-pilot was now turned off. Mary had a new perspective on the big decisions she'd have to make.

Should I Stay or Should I Go?

Should she stay in the corporate world? She felt that, at this stage in her life, she needed to prioritize **Authenticity.** Staying true to herself meant following her vision, not implementing someone else's plan. Self-determination.

So she asked herself, "Can I start a new business? What kind of company would it be? Do I have the financial resources? What about the possibility that it doesn't work out?"

We updated her financial plan and included a worst-case scenario in which the business wasn't successful. After looking at all the angles, we determined that she had the resources to make a major change. We looked up from the paper in front of us, and I said to her, "This is who you are. You go for it, girl!"

While Mary had been an HR executive, really she was a coach and motivator. For 30 years she brought out the best in the talented people she came in contact with. So it was only natural that she transition into executive coaching.

Mary had so many professional colleagues who had become friends over the years. This was her **Community** and could serve as a deep bench for future clients. Other executive coaches would provide encouragement and guidance for her, further growing her community. She had a lot to learn, but **Growth** would come from taking the courses needed for certification.

Authenticity, Community, Growth: Mary's Core Values turned the light green.

You can guess the outcome. Mary completed her coaching certification, brought in clients, and today has a constant smile on her face.

Giving Back

Soon, Mary was asked to join a nonprofit board. We discussed the pros and cons and ultimately, she felt this board position *met all five of her Core Values*. Five for five!

In addition to her board commitment, Mary is donating 150 hours annually of coaching time to help people who otherwise might not be able to afford her services find meaningful work.

Something Was Still Missing ...

With her new career, Mary found her schedule was less structured and she had some extra time in her week. How best could she fill it with something meaningful? While her business offered professional **Growth**, she felt there was room for personal **Growth**. In college, she had always loved literature. She decided to co-lead a lifelong learning class in literature. As a teacher, she'd focus on creating an environment filled with **Respect**.

It All Started with Her Core Value List

Mary's life decisions started with determining her Core Values. When her job was eliminated, she felt apprehension and anxiety about the next stage of her life. She now has more energy than she has had in years.

She recently shared a Theodore Roosevelt quote with me: "Do what you can, with what you have, where you are." We can all learn from this.

I hope this story will inspire you to Maximize Your Return on Life.

MORE MAXIMIZE YOUR RETURN ON LIFE STORIES

Since I have been writing my blog over the past few years, I have received many emails and have had many discussions with clients about Maximizing Their Return on Life. Here are a few of their stories:

Every year **DAVID**'s aunt contributed toward his kids' college savings accounts. David is now at a point in his life with the resources to pay it forward, so he contributes to his nieces' and nephews' college savings accounts.

ASA keeps a tight budget. As her children live out of state, she decided to rent a home in the south of France for a week to spend with her kids and grandkids. It was expensive, but she budgeted for the trip and never looked back. Memories for a lifetime.

PETER AND LINA realized that they were slowing down. Their kids were out of town and they thought it would be helpful to have someone come to the house for a few hours each day to help with errands, cleaning, and home repairs. This was important to them, so they made some adjustments to other expenses. They are happy and so are their children.

MICHAEL AND TALIA were looking at a second home in Arizona. They found a house they loved and Talia realized they would need to reduce their travel expenses to afford the new home. They decided to make the tradeoff. They wanted the home as a destination in which to relax and spend time with their family. It would be a great place for their retirement as well. They went ahead with it, and Arizona became the hub for their extended family. Every time I see them they tell me the latest story about their grandkids. They still set aside money every now and then travel elsewhere—just not as much.

TYLER listened to my advice and made a doctor's appointment. He learned that he needed to lose some weight (okay, maybe he knew that already, but the doctor told him it was serious). He decided to hire a personal trainer and nutritionist. He has lost ten pounds to date and feels great!

MARCUS always wanted to give back to the community. After his retirement from 40 years in corporate America, he ran for public office. He won his election! He enjoys the time he spends as a public servant. A great way to ease into retirement.

EMMA had been a real estate lawyer for ten years. With one child and the long hours both she and her husband worked, it was getting overwhelming. She decided to open her own law firm. Since so many of her friends were having closings, she quickly had a full load of clients. She now feels more relaxed, is able to spend time with her daughter, and enjoys being in control of her schedule.

CAROLINE wanted to teach her grandchildren about investing at an early age. When they started working she told them she would open a Roth IRA and contribute $1,000 for the first $1,000 they earned. She discussed investment options with them. They so appreciated Caroline's gesture and learned about stocks. The extra time with grandma ("investment committee meetings") was an added bonus.

JASON was in the Improv club back in his college days—he loved performing! Now, with a demanding job, he needed an outlet. He looked into a local Improv group and signed up. Not only did he have fun, but he met some new people along the way.

BRANDON had constant guilt when he spent money, even though he was a successful attorney who budgeted carefully. He spent some time looking into his "money beliefs" and realized that he grew up in a home with frugal parents who looked down on any discretionary spending. These thoughts consumed his mind. Realizing the connection allowed him to slowly alleviate the guilt.

DOMINIQUE's youngest child was off to college, and she and her husband were officially empty nesters with some extra time. She had always wanted to volunteer at a local food pantry. She now had the time and decided to try it. She enjoyed it so much, she now goes twice a week.

JOSELYN had always left the finances up to her husband. He always seemed stressed about the markets and seemed to be losing sleep. Joselyn decided to learn more about investing. She quickly realized that their portfolios were not in order. Other major areas, such as estate planning and insurance, had been neglected as well. They were both extremely busy, so she suggested to her husband that they meet with a financial advisor. Joselyn set up the interviews and did the research. They hired an advisor (me!) and feel much more in control of their financial life.

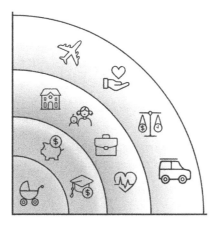

**Every stage of your life has an opportunity to
Maximize Your Return**

EPILOGUE

O NE OF MY FAVORITE MOVIES is *City Slickers.* I love the scene where Billy Crystal's character, Mitch, is alone with Curly, played by Jack Palance. Curly is giving Mitch some life advice.

CURLY:
Do you know what the secret of life is?
(*He holds up one finger.*)
This.

MITCH:
Your finger?

CURLY:
One thing. Just one thing.
You stick to that and the rest don't mean s***.

MITCH:
But, what is the "one thing?"

CURLY:
That's what you have to find out.

As I wrote this book, I also did some soul searching. How would I **Maximize My Return on Life**? I decided to start with "one thing." For me it would be to train for an athletic competition that in my wildest dreams I wouldn't dare to try. A triathlon. No, I'm not kidding!

My quest began at a wine tasting at my friend Elyse's house. After a few sips of wine, I met Libby Hurley. Libby runs Together We Tri, which offers triathlon coaching for beginners (me) all the way up to competitive athletes. Libby told me if I was willing to put in the work, I could do it.

I trained several days each week for six months. Getting up at 5 am for swimming on Saturdays! Tuesday night runs up and down a hillside. Thursday bike rides with a group. I blocked my calendar for the training sessions and made them a priority.

When I started, I could barely swim the length of the pool. A lake swim was a fantasy. I also could not run more than a mile. Would I really be able to complete a Sprint Triathlon (a quarter mile lake swim, followed by a 20k bike ride and then a 5k run)?

With each training session, my confidence grew. I was getting in shape, making new friends with my teammates, and loved being outside training. The lake swims actually became my favorite.

I did it! My One Thing!

I decided to go "dry" in July. No occasional glass of wine.

The night before the race, I had trouble sleeping. I was told later that was normal for first-time triathletes. I left the house at 5:30 am to get situated at the starting line. My adrenaline was kicking in. Before I knew it I was in the lake trying to avoid getting pushed around by other swimmers. But I got through it and ran to where my bike was waiting. My family was at the end of the bike ride, cheering me on.

Now the run. My sister-in-law ran the 5k with me. I was exhausted but she kept me going. Together we crossed the finish line, with Stephen there waiting for me.

What a thrill! I did it. I am now a triathlete.

Your Story

As you go down your own path to Maximize Your Return on Life, here's what awaits.

- Satisfaction from having your time and money aligned with your values.

- Peace of mind that comes from knowing you are protecting your loved ones.

- Confidence from having clarity with your time and money.

- Time to channel your energy into productive and enjoyable pursuits—family, work, community, retirement—knowing that the "money" part of your life is well-planned and on track.

QUESTION

How will you Maximize Your Return on Life?

I'd love to hear your story.

ACKNOWLEDGMENTS

I would like to thank my family, friends, colleagues and clients
who have inspired me to write this book.
It is your stories and your insights
that come to life in each chapter!

Stephen, my husband, life and business partner ~
you have supported me in every way since the day we met.
I am so lucky! As you read each chapter, your "sounds good to me"
sounded so good to me!

Isabel and Maddie ~
you inspire me more than you will ever know
with your energy and passion. You also provided some great material.
Thanks for being such great sports.
You can get back at me when your write your own books.

Mom ~
you moved me along by asking every day "Is the book finished?"
Mom, the book is finished!

Adam Greco, my brother ~
you have always encouraged me to write a book
and share my thoughts with others.
A special thank you to my sister-in-law Wendy,
who posted each blog and read each chapter.

David Rappaport ~
you have truly been a wonderful business partner and friend.
Thanks for your thoughts and edits.
I could not have done this without you!

Karen Asbra ~
thanks for helping behind the scenes
and adding a few touches to each chapter.
Thanks for letting me know if I was "off" base.

Thank you to Laura Szymanski ~
who provided the wonderful illustrations,
Dawn McGarrahan Wiebe at Windy City Publishers for your assistance (and
patience), and to Ruth Beach, who provided additional editing and advice.

Last but not least,
a special shout out to my team at
Rappaport Reiches Capital Management.
I am so fortunate to work with you each day.

The team that helps me
Maximize My Return on Life

ABOUT THE AUTHOR

SHARI GRECO REICHES

S HARI GRECO REICHES brings more than 30 years of experience in wealth management. She is Co- Founder and Chief Visionary Officer of Rappaport Reiches Capital Management (RRCM), which delivers global investment management and financial planning to individuals, families, and non-profit organizations. The firm's *Maximize Your Return on Life Solution* aligns clients' financial planning with their Core Values.

She is a frequent speaker on financial planning and values, author of the *Maximize Your Return on Life* blog, and enjoys mentoring women in the wealth management profession. She has been recognized with the Five Star Wealth Manager award for the past 9 years, and in 2020 was recognized with an appearance in the Women in Wealth section in *Fortune* magazine.

Shari was previously a Board Member and Vice Chair of the Illinois State Board of Investments (ISBI), which manages investments for three Illinois pension funds. She has been active in many civic organizations including the Jewish Federation of Metropolitan Chicago, the Chicago Foundation for Women, The Standard Club, Beth Emet Synagogue, and the Medical Research Institute Council (now known as the Children's Research Fund).

Shari lives in Evanston, Illinois, with her husband Stephen and is very proud of her two daughters, Madeleine and Isabel. Shari enjoys 6 am boot camp workouts with friends, cycling (trying to keep up with her husband), playing bridge, tennis, traveling and spending time with her family. She just completed her first triathlon. Shari also is a Barry Manilow fan (a Fanilow).

Made in the USA
Monee, IL
18 July 2021